P9-AFC-326

DATE DUE

NO 6 97		
AP 6 98		
JY 27 98		
SE 11 98		

DEMCO 38-296

The
POLICE OFFICER'S GUIDE
to
Survival, Health and Fitness

ABOUT THE AUTHOR

John F. Reintzell is a native of Baltimore and a graduate of the University of Maryland and the F.B.I. National Academy at Quantico, Virginia. He is a veteran law enforcement member and a certified instructor who has conducted lectures on Aerobic Fitness, Stress and Nutrition to thousands of police officers. The *Police Officer's Guide* grew out of those lectures.

It grew also from watching the effects police work has on police officers.

The
POLICE OFFICER'S GUIDE
to
Survival, Health and Fitness

By

JOHN F. REINTZELL

CHARLES C THOMAS • PUBLISHER
Springfield • Illinois • U.S.A.

Riverside Community College
Library
MAY '97   4800 Magnolia Avenue
Riverside, California 92506

HV 7936 .H4 R45 1990

Reintzell, John F.

The police officer's guide
  to survival, health, and

Published and Distributed Throughout the World by

CHARLES C THOMAS • PUBLISHER
2600 South First Street
Springfield, Illinois 62794-9265

This book is protected by copyright. No part of
it may be reproduced in any manner without
written permission from the publisher.

© *1990 by* CHARLES C THOMAS • PUBLISHER

ISBN 0-398-05711-7

Library of Congress Catalog Card Number: 90-11245

With THOMAS BOOKS *careful attention is given to all details of manufacturing and design. It is the Publisher's desire to present books that are satisfactory as to their physical qualities and artistic possibilities and appropriate for their particular use.* THOMAS BOOKS *will be true to those laws of quality that assure a good name and good will.*

Printed in the United States of America
SC-R-3

Library of Congress Cataloging-in-Publication Data

Reintzell, John F.
    The police officer's guide to survival, health, and fitness / by
John F. Reintzell.
        p.   cm.
    Includes bibliographical references (p.   ) and index.
    ISBN 0-398-05711-7
    1. Police—Health and hygiene. 2. Physical fitness. 3. Police—
Job stress. I. Title.
HV7936.H4R45   1990
613′ .0243632—dc20   90-11245
                                                                         CIP

For Helen

*

And to the memory of Edward J. Tilghman Sr.,
Police Commissioner (retired), City of Baltimore,
aged 55.

And to the memory of Lt. Charles V. Fertitta Jr.,
Baltimore Police Department,
aged 46.

And to all those gone before their time.

INTRODUCTION

In a recent year past, 78 American Police Officers were killed in the line of duty; another 58,752 were the victims of criminal assaults.[1] Pretty dangerous job? You would certainly think so.

But you might not know the half of it. Because police work kills you from within: not usually with bullets or knives but by the accumulated unrelenting effects of sleeplessness, bad food, and a host of stress-related illnesses.

And this process begins from your first day on the street and continues into retirement, a phenomenon that hacks about thirteen years off your life.

In fact, if I had to *design* an occupation that would ensure bad health I couldn't do much better than the police profession. It has everything: long hours; shift work; exposure to bad weather; unrelenting stress; hurried, often unhealthy meals, or meals skipped altogether; frustrations galore; separation from loved ones (and most of society); lack of opportunity for regular exercise, or physical exhaustion when there *is* time; the threat of communicable disease; alienation; alcohol abuse; sleeplessness, insomnia, or sleep inadequate in quantity and quality; all these and more, and all interacting, usually quietly, to undermine your physical, mental and spiritual health over the length of a career.

I do not overstate these obvious truths because I have lived some of them. More importantly, I have worked with or supervised well over one thousand police officers during my career. The man or woman who can perform well in the police profession *and* retire a healthy, functioning individual is a remarkable and unique person. I've seen a few, but *very* few. Most leave as broken shells with health and/or emotional problems that will dog them the rest of their shortened life spans.

But, of course, you already know all this. Certainly, no one doubts that police work is a dangerous, sometimes fatal occupation. Police injuries from assaults and accidents *are* a very real part of the job; one that even rookie officers are acutely aware of. It's safe to say that relatively few police retirees have not suffered some injury during their careers.

What isn't as widely well-recognized is the fact that the realities of police work—those factors of eating, sleeping, working and recreation—seem to assess far more serious damage to an individual's health than do injuries sustained in the line of duty. These negative effects work insidiously and relentlessly to undermine your health and strength over the span of a twenty-year or so career, rendering even the healthiest entrants into the profession into wasted hulks by retirement age. This harm is amassed cumulatively, year after painful year, until the bright eyes of the newest rookie have been transformed into the exhaustion mirrored in the faces of the often still young, but exhausted retiree.

In most cases, these effects are, at best, difficult to reverse. Premature aging and harmful habituations have taken hold and will continue the work of the individual's destruction, a process which usually ends in premature death.

Some of these negative influences are endemic within our society: a waning but still strong courtship with cholesterol and saturated fats; too much protein, too many cups of coffee and other caffeine products, too much sugar, too little fiber, a total lack of exercise, unrelieved stress and inadequate sleep leading to chronic fatigue; vulnerability to a host of small (later large) diseases.

The greatest tragedy (and irony) in much of this is that **it does not have to be this way.** There is ample evidence available that sensible habits can greatly reduce your risk of impaired health and reduced life span. But the curative effects obviously cannot take hold until you choose to **take charge of your life.**

It sounds simple. But changing lifelong habits is not easy. Habits of eating, sleeping, recreation, and relaxation are fundamental facets of your existence. Their sum total add up to your life-style. They are deeply ingrained and do not lend themselves to easy alteration. Indeed, why should they? After all, these habits are ways you tailored in order to cope with the daily demands of a very harsh working environment. They **work** for you insofar as they have allowed you to survive another tour of duty or another week or year.

And yet, close examination and analysis of your habits will most probably reveal a consistent ignorance about nutrition, exercise, stress reduction and sleep needs, the result of attitude-shaping founded upon inadequate knowledge in your youth and now colored by the less-than-accepting intellectual environment in which you labor. It is an environment that often stifles individual thought, washing most human expression under a coat of macho-induced indifference to suffering and pain, whether yours or somebody else's.

This is stoicism of the most self-destructive type, a futile attempt to ignore your human reactions, emotions and physiology that, at its best, transforms otherwise normal human beings into emotionally and physically impaired individuals. At its worst, playing with pain, of the head or the body; playing despite its pulsations inside of you, consistently, day after day, ultimately cancels your check, noting your funds as insufficient to withstand the damage you have done, or have **allowed** to be done to you. The stoic's reward is an earlier grave and absolutely **nothing** else, unless you choose to weigh the intangibles: a spouse left alone; grandchildren who never got to know you; all the emotional IOU's owed by you to your own children for the missed holidays or shortened or nonexistent vacations; the games and the parties you couldn't attend because of work or sickness, and all the rest of it.

So, having become thoroughly sickened by this terrible and unnecessary waste, here is a guide for survival that, I believe, can contribute a great deal towards the goal of casting off the shroud of ignorance and letting a little light peer through; accepting, in the process, that you are a vital **intellectual** as well as physical being; that your destiny is in your hands and that a little self love can do wonders to heal and counteract what you've already allowed to be done to you.

The process whereby you regain balance in your life cannot take place immediately. Recognizing that primary fact is of utmost importance in turning your life around. Or have you ever seen someone who went on a diet, cut out coffee and snacks, climbed on the wagon and started a rigorous demanding exercise schedule all in the same day? The results were predictable and almost instantaneous: attempting everything at once ensured failure at everything, reinforcing feelings of powerlessness and inadequacy **and** rendering future attempts both distant and less likely to occur.

Life-style changes have to be attempted gradually and usually one at a time over a period of months, even years, to have any realistic chance of becoming accepted and habitual. Abrupt, wholesale changes place far too much additional stress on a body and mind which are probably already stressed quite near their limits of endurance.

A little common sense (an uncommon virtue it sometimes seems) and a little accurate information can go far towards reversing the degenerative health effects of the police profession. This manual is intended to inform and to guide you in your efforts to regain or improve your health. Read it with an open mind. Then map out your strategy. Then begin.

The ensuing chapters constitute an assortment of information concerning you, your body, the effects of your professional and social surroundings, with a dash of insights scattered throughout. Ignorance concerning what are or are not the best ways to eat, drink, exercise and relax can reduce the most sincere efforts to misguided or even harmful exercises in futility, defeating your purpose before you even begin.

Take the time to study these chapters thoroughly, and **first** make connections between your state of health and mind and what you are reading. Then, after reading, absorbing and understanding the second part, set a date and **gradually** begin.

If there is an essential focus to this book, it is this: very little effort on your part can and will produce very startling positive results, very soon. No, your oversized waist is not going to disappear overnight, precisely because that's not how it appeared. And yes, if you are middle-aged or beyond, expect to apply far more patience to your program than your twenty-eight-year-old colleague. Though the human body is a marvelously forgiving organism, its ability to bounce back from years of abuse obviously declines with age. But, it is **never** too late to start . . . until, of course, your loved ones hear your casket click shut.

J.F.R.

ACKNOWLEDGMENTS

The encouragement and support of a number of people vastly assisted me in the preparation of this book. Foremost, I thank Daniel O. Caulk and John C. Lewandowski for their unflagging faith. Mary Lewandowski deserves much credit for her hard work at the word processor and her encouragement as does Linda Wratchford.

Joe Key, Terry Clasing, Susan Stevens, Gary May and Wes Wise each contributed in a unique and very real way. My dear wife, Mary Jane and daughter Debra deserve much credit: they never lost faith that the vessel would drop anchor in a good harbor.

CONTENTS

The
POLICE OFFICER'S GUIDE
to
Survival, Health and Fitness

Chapter I

COPS: MYTHS AND HUMANS

People's perceptions of the police are largely shaped both by media depiction and personal contact. Depiction is usually colored or otherwise distorted to conform to stereotype. Personal contact can and often does take place during incidents that, in greater or lesser ways, try men's souls.

Either way cops are usually looked at through a glass darkly.

Media representation ranges a wide but predictable gamut: from the fatherly characterization personified by **Barney Miller** to the sensitive and tough Commander at the Hill Street Station, Captain Daniel Furillo, to **Dirty Harry**, the cop with the steel eyes.

Personal contact, too, is further tinged with the type of contact: whether it was threatening, supportive, abrasive, efficient or something that somehow combined all these human highs and lows.

It's no wonder, then, that the public's perception of cops is, to say the obvious, rather distorted, particularly when the traditional clannishness and muteness of cops is factored into the equation. And no wonder either that many citizens approach police officers with an almost schizoid sense of fear oddly mixed with admiration, grudging respect and faint distaste.

As human beings you reflect this disparate gallery of views and values. Who you are and how you respond to people's reactions to you explains much about your self-perceptions and your behavior, both as an individual and as a professional.

Let's face it: the job provides enormous potential to accomplish a great deal of good for society. Present also and perhaps more obvious are its numerous potential pitfalls. So it is that every day, somewhere, cops are hailed as heroes or saviors and just as, if not more frequently, criticized as brutal beasts: dishonest, not a little insensitive or stupid, sort of a blowup doll in uniform.

These diverse perceptual distortions, particularly by the media, are especially apparent to your commanders. Not hard to understand why things hardly ever seem to change when you consider the near schizophrenic environment in which most of you **and** your bosses labor. Add to that environment the democratically conceived ordinary man's aversion to authority, uniforms and the like and it becomes clearer why many cops suffer from a distinct identity problem. Where **does** the truth lie?

Implicit in the process of understanding external truths is an understanding of one's self. Members of the profession, I've observed, can be generally differentiated into three groups, two broad, one (happily) narrow; each of which is motivated by a different set of expectations and values:

First, the Type A personality; suffers from **hurry sickness;** attracted by the profession's alleged ends-oriented reputation and its supposed glamor. Upwardly mobile and usually impatient with delay, slow talkers or anything else that looks like less than perfection. Due to their extremely low threshold for frustration and their initially high (and usually unrealistic) expectations, many become burnouts at relatively young ages.

Second, the blue-collar or Type B personality; motivated much less by glamor or the potential for solving problems creatively than by a need to work within a stable (no layoffs) job environment. Probably does not view law enforcement as a profession and usually possesses less motivation to excel through the promotional process than does his Type A colleague. Expecting less, he or she is less inclined to suffer the effects of professional frustration; usually these are the very personification of patience.

Third, the sociopath, or come out from behind those mirrored glasses, partner. An **extremely small percentage** of law enforcement types, but there nonetheless. (**You** know who I mean.)

Characteristics among groups are often **not** mutually exclusive, nor is it impossible for an officer to enter as a Type A and evolve into a Type B or even a sociopath. Further, these groups are not all encompassing: many exceptions can and do exist.

So to find the truth and, more importantly, accept and understand it, let's go back to the time before your entrance on duty. What impelled you then? If you're like most, you genuinely wanted to help people, simple as that. You might also have sought a secure position that was performed in the great outdoors with a minimum of supervision (thinking, you fool you, that no one would be on your case for eight hours a day; that your time would be yours to structure, more or less as you saw fit). Also the uniform, badge, weapon and other gear did not exactly turn you off (be honest now). And you would get respect, at least from most of the people.

So you joined, whether it was a small sheriff's office in a rural county or one of the large urban departments several thousand strong or, like most, somewhere in between in size. And if you received formal training in an academy setting many of your idealistic beliefs were, if anything, strengthened by the training process. Who **were** you? You were the protector, servant and defender of all American society holds dearest (in itself a schizophrenic perception since our society values almost every- thing and nearly nothing); you were the peacekeeper and the role model, the tangible, always available representative of government and you were the one whose presence was most critical whenever little cracks appeared in civilization's micro-thin veneer. Sure you were.

Graduation brought with it a quick splash of reality. Where you had been taught, **this is the way we always handle this,** a fantastic approach to the administration of justice, a corollary to which would seem to dictate that everything in a pluralistic society assorts itself into logical, neat and tidy piles. But then you found out differently, didn't you?

Hitting the street it became apparent to you within a stunningly quick succession of experiences that:

- The public views cops on a par with garbage collectors; at best you're thought of as a talking uniform.
- Sometimes you can't even trust little old ladies who remind you of your aunt.
- Your workday is **somewhat** structured for you by a persona called **Sarge.**
- Some people do not like being arrested. Some even object to the practice.
- If all the lies, distortions and exaggerations you heard each day earned you a quarter apiece, you could be taking in the sun at Cannes while your man buffed your Bentley.
- Respect in our society is not lavishly bestowed upon the peacekeepers, particularly if they wear a uniform.

At the same time as your perceptions are being fine-tuned (at some cost to your self-image), other, equally unsettling lessons were learned. You work shift work and can never seem to get enough sleep, or time off; the carousel onto which you've hopped is revolving too quickly it seems, producing a bewildering kaleidoscope of images, faces and experiences all appearing and receding much faster than you can absorb or comprehend them.

Something has taken charge of your life and has punched holes in the receptacle that held your concepts and values. "It isn't supposed to be like this," thought the yin of you; "Oh, but it **is** like this," answered the yang. You are learning. Make a difference in society? Count for something? **Help** someone? You are finding out with each dizzily passing day that you can't even help yourself: that you have leaped feet first and of your own free will into a whirlwind of such unbelievable force and fury it is sucking the very breath from your body.

And when you turn to family and old friends for a helping hand, some empathy or compassion for the incredible burdens you feel you are bearing, you get blank looks of non-recognition, perhaps a word or two of "It's a new job," they say. Or, "Give it time, it'll get better," they tell you.

And you suddenly, finally realize, "They don't even know what I'm **talking** about": a significant leg of your journey into the land of altered personalities:

> **"He used to be such a lay-back guy before he went with the cops,"** **some of your non-police friends will observe.** Exit non-police friends.
>
> **"Mom, I can't talk to him when he gets like this. He's like another person,"** your spouse will say. Exit spouse?

And, before you realize it three, four or more years have passed. By then the mist is definitely gone from your eyes; the carousel has slowed somewhat (you found the brake right there in your new conscious awareness, under the adage "you cannot be all things to all people all of the time"). Gradually your perceptions have been yanked into reality, including your new self-perceptions. You realize, or are beginning to realize: that police work must be approached as simply just another job, if you are to maintain a slippery hold on your sanity and health; that you will accomplish what you can, but that you are not going to single-handedly rescue our culture from decadence; and that finally, maybe what would set everything right is a change out of uniformed patrol work.

As you, by now, are well aware, it is a firmly established myth that uniformed patrol forces constitute the backbone of any police organization. If that were so, many good cops you see leave to become detectives or other specialists would not be **allowed** to leave, would they? Conversely, burnouts and other confirmed do-nothings from special assignments would not be dumped back into uniform, would they?

Speaking of which, you might not mind trying your hand at a little plainclothes work except there appear to be about a dozen other hopefuls for every vacant position. Never mind, you think, **I'll take the Sergeant's test next year,** only there the odds against you are even worse. The realization, like a jolt of freon injected into your skull comes, icily, unwelcomely: you're not going **anyplace.** You're going to be right here in this patrol car until the day you retire.

"**Why so?**", you ask.

Police departments, like any other labor-intensive bureaucracy, are organized like pyramids: room for lots of doers at the bottom and succeedingly fewer supervisors and command people at each subsequent higher level. And, if you perceive yourself as a partial reflection of that organizational structure, your ego is likely to suffer as a result. So, though you may fervently want, even need, a change to something different, you probably are not going to go any place.

This realization may be accompanied by gastric distress, bitterness or simple stoicism. If you're an upwardly mobile Type A personality, the frustrations bred by professional stagnation produce ego-deflation. This is the career point where many leave the profession altogether. Those who remain often are motivated more by the reality of their debt load and by family responsibilities rather than any vestiges of loyalty to the work itself.

So, that which was viewed as tolerable in terms of your working conditions before, becomes far less acceptable when perceived as an endless progression of days spent doing the same and stretching to a limitless future horizon. It is a phenomenon that creates legions of embittered people trapped by conditions: at best, bored by their work; at worst, despising it.

So, immersed to the eyeballs in a profession that has forever lost its alleged former allure, some cops sublimate, attempting to make the best out of an admittedly bad situation; others take on second jobs to help with expenses that seem to continually grow; some go the alcoholic route, a particularly protracted form of suicide; while many direct their bitterness inwardly in another slow, sustained form of self-destruction, or towards their families and colleagues, further isolating themselves from sources of understanding and help.

"He used to be a good cop," your former partner says. **"But lately I don't even want to be around him."**

Of course, not all feel the frustration and its attendant woes. Those who were attracted to the profession mostly by a need for a secure and stable work environment—yeoman officers capable of, indeed happy, to perform the same tasks over and over for twenty years or so without so much as a change of scenery, can remain genuinely satisfied with their work. Not needing more challenge to feel fulfilled and confident of themselves and their skills, they persevere with eyes consistently held higher than the high tide mark. They are world-beaters in the sense that they have adapted to the ebbs and flows of their chosen profession. Because of this healthy adaptation, they often remain physically healthier individuals than their more self-demanding but often frustrated peers.

Bureaucracy and organizational stagnation compound the natural frustrations which accompany a lack of job mobility. The police profession is not one characterized by creative or progressive administration. And the larger the organization, the more pronounced the tendency. Large bureaucracies resist change the way Winston Churchill fought the Nazis: remorselessly.

The more links in the command/supervisory chain the more decision makers; the more decision makers the less opportunity for fast, decisive action and the more command or supervisory interference in even mundane activities. Trying to get something new accepted in such an environment is like removing a single strand from a bowl of spaghetti without disturbing any other strands. It can be done, but it takes a lot of practice and patience.

To be fair, the modern police administrator is beset with societal conditions that would have scalded the stomach linings of his predecessors. Lawsuits, political interference, a vibrant and sometimes strident press, all of which contribute to his understandable unwillingness to commit an error. Since decisions delayed have far less potential for damaging one's career (you can't be wrong if you don't decide in the first place), potentially controversial decisions are often deferred well beyond the point of perceived professional peril, or even relevance.

This is not to say that progress does not take place, it **does**. However, it does so almost imperceptibly, the way dust accumulates on an end table, or the way you first grew that oversize middle: a very little at a time. Confirmed police bureaucracy observers are the kind of people who get excited watching continental drift; but take heart, things **are** changing. You just can't see it.

What is perceptible almost from career onset are the adverse effects these frustrations can play upon your physical and mental health. Police officers in this country suffer disproportionately from lower back pain, a cause of numerous often job-related early retirements; gastrointestinal disorders; insomnia, high blood pressure (a.k.a. hypertension), ulcers and other related chronic diseases, many of which are psychosomatic in origin, though no less painful for that.[1] And many of these are the direct result of a frustrating, often unrewarding work environment fraught with job stagnation, lack of recognition and minimal opportunity for self-actualization.[2]

The frustrated career officer is like an organism that lives by consuming itself; the end result is an early grave, not usually the result of an armed confrontation with a holdup man, but, rather, slowly and insidiously, damaged cell by damaged cell, adversely affecting the stamina, physical appearance and the strength of the individual as it simultaneously clouds the mind, altering perceptions and personality. Most cops simply die the result of cumulative stresses and frustrations, suffered stoically over too many years. And suffered, more often than not, in abject solitude.

Reconciling the personal realities with the myths of police work can be a devastatingly painful and humbling process, particularly if your views were unrealistically inflated to begin with. Maturation can only result from recognizing the truth and accepting it as the way things are. Successful adaptation to your environment need not entail a lowering of your personal values and standards, but, rather, it demands an adaptation to conditions as you find them. Because you're not responsible for your environment, only your **reaction** to that environment.

Keep in mind also that what appear to be current popularly admired qualities within the American culture often, in retrospect, don't amount to a stack of discarded pizza boxes. The American media feeds on trendiness and bizarre variations of older themes in addition to what pollsters tell them; the significance of occasional off-the-wall occurrences is much inflated when subjected to the scrutiny of a 30-second spot on network news. A steady diet of such aberrant material could cloud anyone's perception. The truth is, traditional values still play an important role in our society, at least as far as the vast majority of Americans are concerned.

Know also that the difficult job you perform has no parallel within our society: indeed there would be no society, nor democracy, without the half-million men and women who comprise our police forces. You guard the frontiers of American freedom as surely as do the armed forces. You are the domestic protectors of our way of life: front-line fighters in a dirty little undeclared war that will never end.

So, if I've painted too dim a picture of your profession and the demands it makes upon you, and if you sometimes feel that your best efforts are often ignored by the public you serve, well the sentiment is a genuine one. And a very old one among the peacekeepers.

No one ever put it better than Rudyard Kipling in a poem he called **Tommy.** Tommy was the perjorative nickname of the nineteenth century British soldier. In the poem, Kipling cleverly criticized the hypocrisy of British society's aversion to their own protectors. In edited version, it goes:

> I went into a public house,
>   to get a pint o' beer
> The "publican," he up and says,
>   "We serve no redcoats here!"
> The girls behind the bar they laughed
>   and giggled fit to die;
> I outs into the street, meself,
>   and to meself says I:
> Well, it's "Tommy this" and "Tommy that,"
>   and "chuck him out, the brute!"
> But it's "savior of his country"
>   when the guns begin to shoot.
> And it's "Tommy this" and "Tommy that"
>   and "Tommy, 'ow's your soul?"
> But it's "thin red line of 'eroes"
>   when the drums begin to roll.

So know the truth because it **will** make you free. And never question your choice of a career. Your choice was a noble one.

Chapter II

SLEEP DEPRIVATION

Consider the role of the police in an increasingly complex society: you are expected to function efficiently at all hours of the night and day, regardless of the nature of what confronts you; decisions made in the instant can and do have mortal consequences far into the future.

The democratic society that demands absolute around-the-clock protection for all is quick to seize upon the well-meaning but unsound decisions of its guardians. Yet, Solomon-like decisions are difficult to expect from members of a profession who are literally sleepwalking through their tours of duty.

A police friend of mine used to kid me about my strict eight-hours'-sleep-per-night rule. **"You're sleeping your life away"** he would chuckle, convinced, I now believe, that his body would continue to function vigorously and forever on the four to five hours a night he was allowing it. And it seemed to work for him: Charlie was an ostensibly vibrant, strong and dynamic sergeant who excelled in the performance of a very demanding job. Unfortunately, Charlie never got to test his theory past the age of forty-two. He died that year, the victim of a heart attack, largely, I believe, due to the long-term effects of inadequate sleep.

The accident that occurred at the Three Mile Island Nuclear Power Plant took place at 4:00 a.m. and involved personnel who had only been on night duty for a few days preceding the incident. For the previous six weeks they had been rotating shifts around the clock on a weekly basis.[1]

It is axiomatic that the law enforcement profession often expects its members to function capably without adequate rest. And yet, few things have such an immediate and adverse impact upon human beings more than do consecutive nights or days without enough sleep. The manifestations are startling: red swollen eyes, impaired psychomotor functions, slurred speech and an inability to concentrate, among many others.[2]

Quality of sleep is generally indicated by five different sleep states: I, II, III, IV, and REM (Rapid Eye Movements). These stages follow each other successively. Research has found that if sleep disturbances occur in

11

either stage II or the REM stage, the quality of sleep will be substantially impaired.[3] Night shift workers attempting to attain quality sleep during daylight hours are much less likely to achieve those deep sleep stages necessary for adequate rest. Part of the reason is environmental: the telephone rings or the kids are playing in the house. But another factor plays a significant role: sound sleeping during the day is more difficult than at night, since the practice violates your biological clock.[4] This is because humans possess something called circadian rhythms.[5] These are naturally occurring parameters of performance which affect all measurable human functions. You, as an individual, exhibit some variation of a daily wave in everything you do. These rhythms are biologically inherent and reflect a subconscious awareness of clock time, regardless of your work schedule.

So, strictly speaking, if you're working midnight and you doze off around 4:00 a.m., it's because your circadian rhythms are being violated. Tell **that** to your sergeant.

Simply stated, inadequate sleep impairs health and efficiency and accelerates the aging process.

And yet, surveillances, court appearances, long stakeouts, frequent overtime and second jobs are an integral part of the profession. Further, the judicial system itself often expects you to finish a midnight shift, be available for 9:00 a.m. court, cooling your heels for hours before your time comes to testify. Then you're expected to perform flawlessly before other witnesses, court officials, a jury and two attorneys, all of whom just had a wonderful night's sleep. You're expected to testify with minimal resort to written notes; be possessed of factual and total recall and field questions fireballed during cross-examination by a well-rested defense attorney.

The fact remains: if you work shift work (and rotating shifts further aggravate the situation) you are not getting the seven or eight hours of sleep a night needed to maintain health.

One researcher concluded that rotating shifts decreased one's life expectancy by five years.[6]

Inadequate sleep accelerates the aging process, but it also does much more. We know this because sleep deprivation research was first done in 1896 and continues to the present day. It's a particularly rich body of scientific research, much of which resoundingly condemns the process of placing humans on a rotating shift basis: give him 14 or 21 days of one

eight-hour schedule, then, just as his body is slowly, torturously beginning to adjust, WHAM! change him or her to a new eight-hour schedule.

Do this for a complete career and you have created something that
looks like a worn-out human being with the intellect and social skills of a
yam.

Shift work, too, places you in a very restricted milieu from society's.
Based on studies of the subject, you become deprived of three essential
elements of physical and psychological health:

1. You cannot ever fully integrate within the larger social order
   because your **time** functions differently than everybody else's.
2. Your family members become torn between the myriad happen-
   ings in the real world and your schedule.
3. Your circadian rhythms combat the mind's efforts to reconcile real
   (i.e. natural/biological rhythms) versus synthetic or artificial shift-
   working realities. Physical and psychological dysfunctions are the
   inevitable consequence.

Negative effects which result, though differing on an individual basis,
have been amply, and scientifically, documented; studies that have
irrefutably linked the impact of rotating shifts to physiological: gastrointestinal disorders and raised serum cholesterol levels.[7] Consistent long-
term instances of sleep deprivation alter eating habits, causing serious
nutritional deficiencies and a host of attendant woes. Also, psychological/
psychomotor problems: i.e. a measurable inability to concentrate, reason
or **make decisions** (of particular interest where police officers are concerned); feelings of anxiety, tension, confusion and depression; to social:
breaking down those very ties with friends, relations, and family that
could potentially ameliorate the most negative effects.

One researcher wrote, "The human system frequently is treated as if it
were a machine and capable of enduring the same load without adverse
consequences at all phases of its circadian rhythm. The modern shift
worker falls victim to this erroneous thinking."[8]

Where there is fatigue there is ample scientific documentation that
short-term memory is poor, unreliable and adversely affected by stress.
Most sensitive to sleep loss were found to be newly acquired skills,
complex tasks and memory requirements. Also, sleep deprivation's effects

are greater in older subjects both with tests that emphasized "speed of performance (Visual Search, Reasoning, Object Usage, e.g.) and those which do not (Auditory Vigilance)."[9]

Also apparent, shift workers suffer from **less** sleep: Morning shift workers average 7.5 hours of sleep; noon workers average 8.5; and night shift workers average only 4 to 6 hours.[10]

These foregoing recount simplistic and predictable physical effects. Rotating shifts, together with the attendant long-term effects of sleep deprivation, combine to make an inherently stressful profession more so. By insidiously reducing an individual's overall physical health and support network it simultaneously reduces his/her ability to cope with the other more visible stressors of the profession, thus reducing the individual's level of health in a perpetual cause-and-effect cycle of bad making worse.

But a mere discussion of the negative effects scarcely affords an adequate understanding of the vast potential for damage manifested in physchological/social contexts. Studies that have dealt with these and the area of motor dysfunction are no less scathing in their denunciations.

"Depressed mental performance during the night hours may be related not only to the circadian rhythms but also to sleep deprivation. When reporting for night duty the shift worker is often **already** tired and sleepy."[11] Even studies dealing with the irreversibility of long-term sleep deprivation effects (retired police officers) showed: "The retired workers ... are more depressive and have more frequent character disorders of an obsessional nature. The differences are sufficiently significant to be retained.... [The retired shift worker] is badly integrated into society and in retirement, when he is able to integrate, has lost the ability to do so. His former working life **has marked him forever** "[12] [italics mine].

As with retirees, so with current workers. Those on rotating shifts reported significantly higher levels of role conflict, lower levels of social support from supervisors and others at work; also the highest scores on boredom, dissatisfaction with work loads and overall dissatisfaction with their jobs.[13]

Other studies concluded that "behavioral tasks have a tendency to show decline with deprivation of sleep; psychological and emotional parameters do so even more consistently and dramatically. Several studies show increases in depression, anxiety, confusion and fatigue."[14]

And what of the adverse effects on family and the individual's social ties? Although the occupational medical community considers the physiological problems related to shift work of primary concern, shift workers themselves feel that **psychosocial** difficulties create the greatest problems in their lives. Thus, they are more concerned with whether shift work will interfere with or disrupt family relations or their social lives.[15] The result: much of the difficulty of coping with shift work is transferred to spouses and children.[16]

Studies' results of the solutions are no less salient. "Under conditions of a **stabilized** night shift system, in which the hours of work and rest are the same each day, a clear improvement of performance in calculation and vigilance are observed."[17] Though sleep during the day still differs from night, "profile analysis pointed to grouping individuals into morning alert/evening tired . . . to morning tired/evening alert."[18] Adaptation was found to be more acceptable "in **fixed** rather than rotating shifts." Another researcher contended "steady nightwork enables the daily rhythm to be adapted better . . . than that which can be achieved between day and night shifts. . . . "[19]

These represent only the most esoteric of considerations. Consider the sleep-deprived officer operating an emergency vehicle in all conditions of weather and lighting. Are his judgment and abilities impaired to the extent that he constitutes a threat to the citizens he serves? Have these effects, for years, contributed to accident-frequency rates? Are they somehow contributing to medical-leave usage, alcohol abuse, marital separations and divorce rates? Are they a factor in apprehension and clearance rates? Or do they contribute to a suicide rate among police officers higher than most other occupations?[20]

I can't demonstrate that a direct cause-and-effect relationship exists in **all** of these instances. However, the research cited most certainly indicates the enormous potential for harm that exists. Shift work inhibits efficiency and good performance and is a well-documented source of physical and mental harm.

So if you're in poor physical shape and declining health to begin with, the negative effects of inadequate sleep will be accelerated, as will be the process of aging.

Obviously as I contend throughout, many of the demands of this profession can be very harmful, even eventually fatal, particularly as they interact to wear down your mental and physical health. Sleep deprivation, far from being the exception to the rule, is a unique debilitating factor because, I believe, no other single adverse effect is so **universally suffered** nor so consistently harmful. It is the foundation upon which all succeeding stressors and negative impacts are layed; touching every element of your life it makes every negative thing you're suffering inestimably worse. Further, inadequate sleep excludes no one from its pathological grip; indeed, its severity deepens as you age, assessing, finally, the cumulative and irreversible impacts that reduce healthy young men and women into hollow human shells.

Chapter III

STRESS

Describing police work, a writer on the subject called it one of the most emotionally dangerous jobs in the world. Beyond the realm of bullets and barricades, however, which **are** rare occurrences within the profession, lies a region of terrible tedium and mindless repetition, occasionally punctuated by terror: a succession of mundane morality plays, each spun out to its usually predictable conclusion, and each with a sequel in production for tomorrow or next week.

Depending on which expert you read, police work is or is not a highly stressed profession, staggering under epic rates of suicide, alcoholism, divorce, and a wide range of psychosomatic disorders or it is merely one of many highly stressed occupations and not very high on the list at that.

What might appear contradictory actually casts a significant illuminating beacon on the subject of stress, for stress cannot be too narrowly defined, no more than can be any group of human beings, each one possessed of a multitude of emotions, perceptions, biases, quirks and coping techniques. Humans are obviously complex creatures and to generalize concerning the experiences of a group of them is to do disservice to the individuals who comprise the group.

Stress is as highly personalized as any environmental influence, since there are unlimited numbers of human perceptions. And though the many manifestations of stress can be and have been delved to a large extent, the true interpretation of its effects remains as elusive as a definition of the human spirit. On the one hand, stress has been described as a catalyst that facilitates the process of emotional growth. Conversely, it is also recognized as a kind of psychic toxin that can and does poison both the mind and the body, even unto the death of its victim. Interestingly, both descriptions are accurate.

So little understood is the true nature of stress, most researchers have contented themselves with producing studies which measure the symptoms, both physical and mental, stalking as they did so the periphery of the tall

17

grass where their quarry lies; producing through this process, well-intentioned, occasionally fascinating, but usually limited insights.

Dr. Hans Selye was the first to describe the general adaptation syndrome consisting of three coordinated phases mobilized by the body to adjust to an environmental change that is perceived as a stressor:[1]

Alarm Reaction— perception that there is an attack upon the body and mobilization of physiological defenses; the pulse quickens, lungs take in more oxygen to fuel the muscles, blood sugar is elevated, pupils dilate, digestion slows and perspiration (as in your palms) increases. The body is now geared for either fight or flight.

Resistance— maximum adaptation to perceived threat. The body begins to repair the damage done by the arousal and the stress caused symptoms begin to dissipate **unless the stressful situation continues;** if that occurs exhaustion will set in; bodily functions will slow and **continued exposure to stress will result in disease. Those organs predetermined by heredity, life style and diet to be the weakest, will break down first.**

Exhaustion— the adaptive mechanisms collapse from the effort. Bodily functions slow to normal or even sub-normal.

It is believed that personality can contribute much to an individual's harnessing and regulating these phases: using them, in essence, to his or her maximum advantage while minimizing the physiological harm done. Obviously such a healthy adaptation takes place only in the presence of previous experiences; a consequent understanding of the physical manifestations elicited by a stressor and reinforced by good nutrition and regular exercise; a healthy life-style, in short.

Selye's syndrome is useful as a set of descriptors more or less common to humans in the face of danger or some other stressful event, the kind which doesn't occur too frequently over the length of a police career. Holdup-in-progress calls (and driving to them through traffic at 70 m.p.h.) are a good example, what I would call a grand mal stressor and one pretty universally perceived as such. Though they are an intrinsic part of the job, it's probably a rare occurrence to experience, at most, a few a week and in quieter jurisdictions that frequency of occurrence is usually far lower. With even minimum adaptation, comprehension and health levels, these relative few instances of high stress are not remotely health-threatening in and of themselves.

It is at this point, however, where police work and work-related stresses diverge from the norm of society's, insofar as cops are consistently exposed to scenes most folks don't ever see even in their worst nightmares: accident victims, maimings, arsons, murder, pools of human blood, suicides, abused children (and worse, infants), and more: corruption, poverty, human degradation and genuine despair. Taken together, the cop experiences a daunting catalogue of negatives about human existence; (Have you ever forgotten the first corpse you came upon?); enough to transform the most robust optimist into a mountaintop-dwelling hermit.

At best these experiences turn you cynical about mankind. At worst you **become** a cynic, forever failing to see any of the world's obvious beauty or any of the good in your fellow human beings. This condition develops over time, years actually, the product of constant exposure to the petit mal stressors of the street few, if any of which, produce the alarm reaction stage: no sweating palms or dilated pupils, just a growing sense of helplessness that, untreated, degenerates finally into giving up and going through the motions, wearing your macho cop mask for emotional protection and not just while you're at work.

How is it that cops, mostly above average in intelligence and in good health at career outset, find it so difficult to successfully adapt to the tawdry conditions they occasionally find within our society? Why does constant exposure to so many relatively small, predictable occurring traumas or tragedies contribute to degenerating a cop's health, finally extinguishing the bright flame of idealistic outlook and youthful expectations? (Old-timer overheard to rookie: **"There ain't no good days. Just days."**)

Several interdependent factors are at work here. In order for a situation to be stressful it must first be **perceived** to be so by the individual.[2] And stress effects can be lessened, according to research, if a person believes he or she can **control** their role within the stressful situation: notice, not control the **situation**, but **their role**.[3]

Most cops are males; indeed, the majority of cops are firstborn males or the only male offspring of their family.[4] Perhaps it is a male trait or a widely recognized essential element of the police profession. The male cop feels he must be in **absolute control** of every situation he encounters. To lose control is to lose masculinity, not to say face. But obviously no one can be in total control of every situation, so this essential element approach to policing is as hopelessly flawed as it is thoroughly ingrained: a classic no-win hypothesis that contributes a great deal towards creating internalized stress.

But flawed or not, the take-charge element is, as you know, absolutely **expected** of you by the folks who pay your salary, many of whom display woeful ignorance of the existence of things like the Bill of Rights. ("**Well**

why can't you search him if you think he's got pot?," they ask you. And you try to patiently explain, ever mindful that if **they** were the object of your investigative attention the constitution would instantly re-emerge, looming over your efforts like the faces at Mt. Rushmore.)

Add to these factors the written and verbal strictures of the Department for which you labor, each directive tending more to circumscribe rather than clarify the extent of your authority and discretion (and each of which might begin: "Thou shalt not . . . "), pouring from the presses in large departments like an irresistible flood, producing manuals as hefty to tote as they are injurious to your initiative and drive, and you have upped the stress levels considerably.

Thus, the cop who once perceived himself as primary doer within the drama of life sees day by day that he is more a manipulated puppet than man of action; a pathetic creature enmeshed in a sticky bureaucratic web, across which he can maintain **some** mobility and freedom of action but only with great and unceasing effort. It is a portrait of protector turned victim.

Ultimately, stress of the enervating petit mal type is a disease caused by frustration; the sum total of all the emotional abrasions you suffer over the length of a career, and the widening gap between how you perceive yourself as a cop and how others (significant others, to be sure) view you: baby-sitting prisoners in the hospital; serving summonses; acting as a security guard for a favored merchant. Unpromotable, unmovable and finally unmoved by all that engulfs you. Frustration ultimately that even your best efforts cannot hope to stem the rising tide of the muck that seems to envelop everything.

So ultimately you perceive: If there's health to be had by merely controlling your role within each situation you encounter, then so be it. Controlling your role becomes a fallback defensive position, a psychologically sandbagged bunker that distances you from the scenes of frustration and softens the pain of frequent disappointments.

How much of the pressure is self-imposed through Type A behavior and how much is externally imposed is a highly personal matter **and** an issue not even answerable by most individuals. To many, entering their bunker is a conscious, deliberate and rational act; a psychological trimming of the sails and a decision to retard the rate of daily stresses before the daily stresses retard them. High expectations for one's performance and potential for growth get knocked down a notch or two during this process, but no major harm is done and at least the pace is slowed somewhat, providing time to breathe and consider one's relative place amidst the tedium or the turmoil.

And if adjustment to real conditions results, so much the better; you have adapted, coped with your stressors and emerged, if not triumphant, then certainly intact and ready to sally forth once more.

Unfortunately for many, the conscious (or subconscious) act of entering the bunker becomes a progressively stronger motivating influence: an "if some is good, more must be great" perspective begins to assert itself as the sandbags are systematically removed and replaced with four-inch armor plate. Your psychological defense is now capable of surviving a direct hit. Welcome to burnout.

Social scientists refer to burnout as an inappropriate response to stress.[5] It occurs when an individual's resources are overwhelmed by the demands imposed by his environment. Ironically, it often affects the overcommitted, overcaring cop, replacing his initial zeal with apathy and exposing, in the process, a significant insight or two into the burn-out victim.[6]

Burnout as a coping mechanism is a little like death: your mind is telling your body to slow down (as opposed to real death when nature tells you the same thing, one last time). As such it is a last-ditch kind of defense, an armored hull of invulnerability that protects but, at the same time, dramatically limits your ability to enjoy **anything** on or off the job. It is a stiff price to pay and an unnecessary one.

But it does instruct about the individual. Perhaps he loved himself too little to really notice what was happening to him. Perhaps he could not slow the carousel, step back and analyze a life and work style that was self-destructive (and destructive to his family as well). Or perhaps he believed, as many people do, that his innate strengths were sufficient to see him through **any** combination of the forces arrayed against him. And as for stopping, maybe smelling a wildflower along the way—merely because it is beauty and it's there, **"You've got to be kidding—I got three kids and two jobs; always in court. . . . "** Well, there's simply no time for that.

So the burnout victim slams shut the hatch and retires in place, doing enough to get by and determined to ride it out until pension time; letting colleagues take up the slack, becoming in the process some of the litter on the professional landscape: of little good to the public, his department or himself.[7]

Burnout can and does occur at any age, not surprising in a profession where, generally speaking, excellence is expected, not rewarded.[8] The high-achiever who enters such an environment determined to handle everything thrown at him better than its ever been handled **and** ask for more; adamantly maintaining that an individual can make a difference to mankind but foolishly ignoring that minute portion of humanity which includes himself, his family and friends, dances, in his ignorance and arrogance, upon a very high catwalk indeed.

And it is not a performance that long goes unnoticed by colleagues and family members. Numerous symptoms grouped by emotional, behavioral and physical manifestations will usually, in some combination, surface and precede his nosedive.[9]

In addition to apathy, other emotional symptoms include anxiety, fatigue, irritability and defensiveness. In some instances outright hostility is displayed towards supervisors and other colleagues. And though the progression of emotional changes can become manifest in several ways, what remains significant is that noticeable change has taken place **for no other apparent reason.**

Behavioral indicators are somewhat less difficult to notice: neglecting ordinary responsibilities; alcohol abuse; promiscuity or carelessness in cleanliness or personal appearance, to name a few.[10]

Then, what begins as a personal resource deficit, if unchecked, invariably degenerates into physical ailments and not only among those victims past the stage of burnout, but all those who choose to stoically endure rather than ameliorate the causes of the stress.[11] The physical being, already weakened through years of inadequate rest, poor eating habits, lack of exercise and chronic worry, readily succumbs to the first wave of disorders, be they colds, headaches, insomnia, weight gain or loss, indigestion, nausea, vomiting, diarrhea or others. Here the disease begins the process of debilitation, slowly sapping strength and vitality from the victim; in effect prepping his body for incursion by more serious ailments.

Allied with his apathy and his stoicism, the little ills usually go ignored or receive the barest minimum of treatment. But treatment, even when sought, often only deals with symptoms, not causes. And in the meantime, his health continues to steadily, often imperceptibly, deteriorate. It is a fact: two-thirds of all cops' visits to doctors result from

stress-related illnesses.[12] The mind and the mind's perceptions do, in fact, rule the body, just as stress has been amply demonstrated to increase one's susceptibility to disease.

Indeed, research has shown that many disease-causing microorganisms indigenous to our environment can **only** establish themselves **and** exert pathological effects in persons suffering under conditions of **prolonged psychological stress.** [13]

The list of disorders and diseases believed intrinsically related to stress is a comprehensive one and includes such outright killers as heart attack, cancer and hypertension; life-degrading ones like diabetes, bronchial asthma and tuberculosis; gastrointestinal disorders: irritable gastritis, spastic esophagus, colitis and peptic ulcer; musculoskeletal ailments: lower back pain and cramping, to mention a few. Even skin-related problems including hives and herpes are believed to be related to stress.[14]

Researchers have theorized that this relationship between stress and disease is caused by the body's autonomic response to stress which Hans Selye first identified. When coping is only partially successful in defending against the stressor, the body retains abnormally high levels of hormones; adrenaline, for example, but specifically the glucocorticoid group that includes hydrocortisone and cortisone, both of which are believed to inhibit the body's production of disease-fighting antibodies, also decreasing the production of white blood cells which ward off infections.[15]

What does all that mean? It means your immune system, your very first line of defense against infection and disease, **simply doesn't work right.** So your body's antibodies can't cope with little invasions called colds or the more serious incursion called cancer.

Implicit in all the degenerative physical and mental processes is the effect of perception. It runs like a common thread through the total fabric of stress. This is not to say that all perceptions are accurate or even objective. They are not, originating, as each does, within a complex human mind. Even in isolation human perceptions of the same occurrence can differ significantly. When group dynamics enter the equation, particularly the self-protective group instincts of cops, perceptions can and are altered to conform to group expectations, sympathies and biases.

Additionally, the requisites of a male-dominated subculture generally serve more to circumscribe, rather than amplify, those stressors affecting the group. Specific perceived instances of individual weakness or vulner-ability, stemming from even legitimate cause, must be concealed from the group lest the stressed one be willing to add ridicule and threat of rejection to his original worries. Thus, the potential for real support from the officer's immediate peers is greatly limited by the consensual mores of the group. This is obviously an inadequate outlet since it forces the individual to always maintain most of his stoicism, submerging and concealing his true feelings and legitimate concerns from his colleagues.

Though the enormous pressures thus created are tacitly recognized by individual members, the group consciousness oftentimes displays less than the sum total of its members' collective sensitivity. Some subjects are okay to discuss and some are not. Added to this inherent group inadequacy to assist its members in their need to cope with all stressors is the fact that most group-sponsored coping techniques are, at best, mal-adaptive and, at worst, downright destructive. And the officer, to retain membership in the group, is usually expected to participate.

Since the preeminent form of relaxation and stress reduction often centers around the consumption of alcohol, group drink-a-longs to relieve tensions often contribute to the creation of additional stressors for the members who, thus, further impair their perceptions and senses; further estrange themselves from their families (due to their absences); and further degenerate their physical capability to cope with **tomorrow's** stress, not to mention running the risk of a D.W.I. arrest while weaving their way home.[16]

So, while the informal group thus largely abrogates its role as the reducer of many significant stressors for its members, simultaneously it adds to their potential woes by encouraging the abuse of alcohol; and by superimposing its collectively perceived threats **to the group** on him or her (who might or might not care less when considered just from an individual's perspective); and by imposing a set of expectations to cir-cumscribe freer communication which inhibits individual behavior.

At its worst the informal group can run counter to every other element in the officer's life: his family, his department, his moral values and his own health. Though this is admittedly a rare set of circumstances, the worst characteristics of human group behavior **will** generally outweigh the positive aspects.

Over the long haul of your career, adherence to informal group-imposed standards of communication and behavior will increase your sources of stress and decrease your freedom of expression and action to successfully cope with the sources of that stress. For stress to be adequately identified and dealt with, it must first be accurately perceived.

When the unrelenting pressures within an individual cannot adequately vent at work: departmental strictures; in the informal group: risk of ridicule or worse, ostracism; in play: **"who the hell's got time to play?"** or in any other corner of the sufferer's environment, they will explode in the place least prepared and least deserving of the detonation: his home.

Here, too, perceptions and expectations again play a significant role. Home is where you should be able to exert and enjoy a measurable amount of influence over your surroundings. Home is where, normally, you retreat for solace, support, comfort and relief from the harshness of the world. You **expect** certain things to be the way you want them to be. After all it's **your home,** isn't it?

The spouse and children who cannot share your working days with you; who cannot comprehend the abrasiveness of your working environment (who, in fact, have been **protected** from those harsh realities by **you**) cannot hope to be other than ignorant concerning the conditions that are harming you.

And you (by now conceding that you can't really have an impact on conditions within the larger environment), working midnight and trying to sleep during the day and awakened twice, mind you, by the laughter and squeals of your kids playing outside or by the phone or a delivery man or traffic, come to the infuriating conclusion that you can't even control the environment where you live.

This realization, which comes early in most police marriages, is a maddening one which can engender dark feelings almost akin to betrayal. Resentment is the inevitable result, laid like a lash across the back of your unsuspecting spouse.

It manifests itself variably; in silence, the decent man's way of inflicting cruelty on a loved one; in bickering, finding fault, constant expressions of displeasure and disappointment; with absences, perhaps, which grow in duration and frequency.

Here then, at home, you recognize, is the ostensibly safest site for you to vent some of the poison inside you, no matter what the complaint: money, the kids, her parents, sex, the roof, the plumbing, no topic's too broad nor too trivial for you to throw in the face of your spouse. Maybe you **are** feeling a little trapped, boxed-in, like a white rat worrying through a maze filled with sharp turns and blind passageways, always coming back to the beginning, always hoping there's a way out.

So, fueled sometimes by alcohol or impelled by sleep deprivation or your nascent ulcer or your lower back pain, you take on your family; intoning a litany of your demands and disappointments, all the time repressing or ignoring the real source of your frustrations and aggressive behavior.

Your spouse, only dimly aware of the stressors under which you labor and faced with the specter: you vs. your former self, blanches first, then fights back; the children too, when they're old enough in an unending series of skirmishes or worse, silences that crush tender feelings, sunder affections and ultimately serve only to further remove you, the sufferer, from your first, last and best source of solace and support: your family.

Not all can or do direct their explosions at the family. Some choose merely to suffer in silence, bottling up the more expressive form of emotion and trying to carry on as though all is perfectly normal.

Masking their feelings, whether behind a bland countenance or an excessively animated one, they are walking time bombs, ticking not-so-merrily away, perhaps even believing that stressors ignored are stressors defused. Though they represent the greatest potential for violence, the shock, when it comes, is as likely as not to be inwardly directed, a kind of silent implosion that will manifest itself in some virulent form of self-destructiveness.

Suicide or attempted suicide are the most obvious manifestations, but there are others, less identifiable as sustained stress channelled inward: bleeding ulcers; alcoholism; accidents; a penchant for injuring oneself; obesity and more.

Each is a statement by its individual author of two things: a cry for release (and assistance) together with a self-loathing and a self-perception of unworthiness.

Andy (obviously not his real name) was a middle-aged cop with over twenty years invested on the job. One payday he used ink eradicator to remove the computer-typed net amount from his paycheck, substituted, with a manual typewriter, a figure a few hundred dollars more and proceeded into a bank on his post, in uniform, to cash his altered check. The alteration was so bad even a child would've spotted it. The teller took the check to the manager who called the police. The police came, looked at the

check and locked up the check-passing cop. **End of job. Another dumb, dishonest cop made into history.**

At the time it occurred the investigating officers couldn't believe such an amateurish attempt. In retrospect, was the check-passing a way of relieving the pressure? Just as those you hear about arrested for drunk driving or shoplifting or for assaulting their spouse. Because when an individual perceives that all his channels of release are tamped tightly shut, no way to turn for help, no exit in sight, then his behavior can veer off-center and proceed by a seldom-trod path toward some form, any form, of blessed relief.

If there is a saving grace amidst this turmoil it is cop humor. It functions like a bleeder valve: useful in allowing minute amounts of pressure to escape. Seldom mistaken for subtlety it has at least evolved from heydays that saw the promiscuous use of itching powders, exploding cigarettes, saran-wrapped toilets and the like. Whoopee cushions, too, have mercifully also become passe' (at least in most jurisdictions).

Some examples:

Nicknames: Aggressive Street Cop — Genghis Khan
Short Blonde Officer — The Smurf
Pre-pubescent Female — A Bimbette
Short Stocky Officer — R2 D2
Authoritarian Sergeant — The Ayotolleh
Locker Room Graffiti: (about swarthy, shaggy-maned officer)
"Frank R: living proof the Indians married buffalo!"

Psychologists recognize other universally adapted coping mechanisms that people use, usually without even being conscious of doing so. They are employed by a person who has perceived a threat to his self-identity and whose psyche turns to one or more of these devices to dodge that threat. Like antacids, however, coping mechanisms only give a kind of temporary and deceptive relief: while fending off the threat, they ignore the central problem. Among them are:[17]

- **Repression**— Keeping undesirable thoughts out of your conscious mind—a kind of psychological erasure of anything that threatens one's identity.

- **Rationalization**— Altering undesirable thoughts, wishes, memories or impulses into something more acceptable and/or desirable, consistent with your self-image.
- **Projection**— Avoidance of threat to your ego by relocating the impulse. or trait, unloading it on another person.
- **Denial**— refusing to accept the existence of undesirable thoughts, wishes, memories or impulses.
- **Isolation of affect**— Repressing the emotional aspects; emotional insulation.
- **Regression**— Avoiding undesirable feelings by reverting to a previous stage of maturity.
- **Compensation (Overcompensation)**— Making up for a real or imagined defect by creating a real or imagined superiority.
- **Repentance**— Atoning for and thus counteracting the effects of past undesirable acts.

If you've never noticed any of these devices used by the people who populate your environment, then you're not paying attention. In point of fact, you see most of them used every day of your life.

In many ways these mechanisms represent the fantasy picture of the real world created by its adult inhabitants and sometimes its children, too; behavioral manifestations that aid in coping with the abrasions of the world which simultaneously keep one's self-perceived identity intact.

Like the psychology of the male-dominated group, these coping mechanisms also inhibit true communication between ourselves and others. Ironically, while reducing the effects of a stressor for the user, they can create and greatly heighten stress for the recipient. For example, **emotional insulation**:

> You: **"Good morning, Sarge!"**
> Him: **"Don't start on me, dork."**

Thus it is that our perceptions, social interactions and inappropriate or ineffective means of adapting to stress all combine to make an inherently stressful profession much more so. And stress as you have seen and as you have suffered it is a potentially lethal malady: past a certain point its ill effects are cumulative and irreversible. Alone it can and does raise serum cholesterol levels, aggravating conditions of high blood pressure, contributing to incidents of heart attack and stroke and a host of other serious ailments.[18]

Stress untreated not only shortens your life it also strongly contributes to diminishing the quality of that life.

The antidote to this deadly condition is ostensibly a simple one that resides within each of us: personal growth, a steady, intelligent and comprehensive set of outlooks and attitudes, rationally conceived and reasonably founded that can effectively reconcile your perceptions with the realities of your world. This process demands that an individual take charge of his or her life, balancing personal demands with personal resources and recognizing that overload is a disease of the overcommitted, over-caring individual, **and that it can only come from within you.** [19]

It is a crowning paradox of the profession that it demands a healthy attitude from its members in order that they be able to withstand all that a variegated society can heap upon them, and yet most bureaucracies often serve to dismantle that healthy attitude, outlook by outlook, from a member's very first day, either through chronic over-regulation, or by the insidious impact of its informal organizations.

The individual caught up in this process who denies himself the time to analyze and prioritize his environment, then act accordingly, has deprived himself of a higher purpose to life and to the living of it.

Chapter IV

BODY AND HEALTH

PHYSIOLOGY: THE COMPONENTS OF YOU

If there's a more adaptive or complex organism on this planet than the human body it hasn't come to light yet. Your body, that's the thing below your mouth that you've taken for granted all these years, is a veritable marvel of design and engineering. It can and does accomplish miracles of strength and endurance; it is a model of adaptation; a product of hundreds of thousands of years of evolution. It survives unbelievable abuse from most tenants and astonishingly, given half a chance, it can usually heal itself of most ills. Given half a chance, that is.

It's a sad but accurate commentary: most Americans treat their cars far better than they treat their bodies. Cars have monthly payments and are a significant part of the American life-style. Bodies are free, so most of us tend to take them for granted.

The problems usually start when your inner odometer clicks past 100,000 miles or so, (around age 40) and you begin to realize that you can't get a new warranty. Or a new body.

Human beings were designed to walk across continents and perform hard physical labor from morning until lights out. The technology of our modern times, however, has made it unnecessary for most of us to perform hard physical work and our affluent society and productive farmers have made it possible for us to stuff our faces with the enormous bounty of this land. A sedentary life-style plus nightly seconds at the bacon and cheeseburger chapel equals a nation of beach ball smugglers, waddling through the supermarket aisles of life.

Few professions are more sedentary than police work. Stated more simply, police work often requires you to sit on your posterior for long periods of time, waiting for someone to screw up or the radio to summon you. Certainly there are periods of intense physical exertion: foot chases, wrestling with a suspect, etc., but these, as you know, are **exceptions** to the rule of your eight-hour shift.

The particular disgrace of this is that most departments have minimum standards of physical fitness that an applicant has to meet before joining. Police recruits are probably the healthiest of any professional group in the country.[1] Going in, that is. In the absence of physical performance standards throughout a career, your body begins to sag and bulge; flights of stairs get steeper; purse-snatchers seem quicker and more agile, until just changing a tire on a warm day can bathe you in your own sweat and cause your pulse to rocket dramatically.

Fatty meals, no exercise, sleep deprivation and addictions combine to tear down the body's defenses, accelerating the aging process—making you old and vulnerable well before your time.

Doctor William Kroes, writing about this phenomenon in **Job Stress and the Police Officer,** observed of cops: "They are healthy men. Strong men. Yet, year after year we see them struck down at comparatively young ages when early health history would seemingly point to above average longevity."[2]

The shame of this lies in the fact that the human body, unlike most machines, actually **thrives** on being used frequently and hard. The harder you work your body, the **stronger** it becomes. Conversely, allow your body to lapse into long periods of inactivity, it weakens, sickens and suffers the effects of premature aging.

Ever notice police retirees who come back to the station to visit their still working cop friends? Usually they are pitiful wrecks of humanity because, unwittingly, they allowed the peculiar pitfalls of the profession to rob them of their youthful vigor. Many were already old men by their mid-forties. And by retirement age they had become mere specters of their former selves. Unfortunately, in most instances, it's too late for them to reclaim strength or vigor.

The cumulative effects of ignoring health assessed an exorbitant cost. **Yes,** the body can take it and still bounce back given the chance, but there is a point, different for each of us and quite possibly packaged in some genetic code and that code determines a point in time when these harmful effects become irreversible.

In-service standards of physical fitness are often given a lot of lip service, and little else, by most police agencies. The trip wire to ensuring that fitness standards are attained might be employees' organizations;

apathy or ignorance on the part of chief executives (though surely this is changing as the country has become more fitness conscious); the non-availability of suitable facilities; or the laziness of the individual.

Implicit in this tug-of-war lies a fundamental element. Good health and fitness not only make you feel better and look younger, they also improve job performance, productivity and **survivability** in the event you are seriously injured on the street.

Several years ago I listened to a veteran law enforcement member describe the how and why of a serious attempt made on his life by two armed assailants while he lay asleep in his bed, in his home. A dedicated physical fitness enthusiast at the time of the attack and now, he sustained two serious gunshot wounds and actually died; once at his house after paramedics arrived, later on the operating table; but was resuscitated each time. After recuperation he was told without reservation by the operating physician that he **would** have died (the usual way: permanently) had he not been in such superb physical shape. His extremely healthy body was able to counteract the trauma of gunshot wounds and huge blood loss, injuries that would have killed the average person, proving that the well-tuned body is a medical marvel and real good insurance for a working cop. Because, as you know, there are times when the only thing you have to depend on is you.

How many cops do we bury each year who could have survived attacks if they'd been fit? I don't know the answer, either, but even one would be far too many, wouldn't it?

Beyond these provocative considerations, however, there remain the less dramatic concerns of daily living. When was the last time you really **felt** good, as in alert, vibrant, lots of energy, your senses taking in every whiff and hue, every tactile stimulation and melody of your environment?

Physical fitness and overall health dramatically heighten your awareness of your world and greatly improve your ability to think and to know; to recall and to analyze; to enjoy what you hear and see and feel and taste. The veil of dulled senses that descends around the chronically tired, malnourished, understimulated, unexercised self is a self-imposed graying of the world made more insidious because in most cases it has come upon you in nearly imperceptible stages.

At its worst you don't even really understand what has happened to you, only that everything seems bland, colorless, like a pastoral land-scape done in black and white and hung in a dark corner of the gallery.

This malaise robs you of most of the beauty, sensations and sensuality of life. And you don't even know, many times, that you are suffering.

And, as it robs the individual, it steals from your employer, begetting a dull-witted slow-thinking cop, stumbling through his tour of duty, incapable of distilling from the multitude of daily impressions and perceptions that essence of what is critical: the single blond hair imbedded in blood at the possible scene of a homicide; what he had in his hand as he turned towards you, a flashlight? a revolver? The hidden or deliberately distorted facts in your prime witnesses' statement.

Yes, life can be lethal, certainly confusing unless you know where to look and how to listen; and if your senses are practiced, attuned and in **good working order,** which, if you're out of shape they are incapable of being! So, you shuffle through your days, dim-witted, discerning a small percentage of all the stimuli that targets you, robbing your employer, under-protecting the public that depends on you for their all and, perhaps most sadly, cheating yourself out of a better quality of life.

Worst of all, knowing that something should be done to correct these conditions, you look for help outside yourself or you blame your work schedule, your spouse, your boss, your department, your parents, your president, your family and friends, your doctor, your progeny or your predecessors, missing, in each accusatory swipe of your index finger, the real wrong doer: you.

The body is a structure all of whose parts must be in balance to function well. It consists of interrelated systems and substructures where, quite often, an injury or illness in one part adversely affects the whole. Some very important components include:

The Heart and Blood Pressure — the human heart is another engineering marvel that performs prodigious labors all of your life, beating (an average of) 72 times per minute, 24 hours a day. Each compression forces about three ounces of blood into the arteries. That's nearly seven quarts a minute. The heart's only rest from all this activity is **between** beats since the contracting segment takes up only about 40 percent of the heart cycle.[3]

Two pressures are exerted during the cycle: diastolic occurs when the heart relaxes and the ventricles are filling with blood, preparatory to their being emptied into the arteries; systolic pressure is exerted at the time of contraction.

In a blood pressure of 120/80, the larger figure represents pressure during contraction while the smaller figure is the pressure exerted when the heart is at rest. This latter figure, then, is the more critical of the two since it measures the pressure exerted on the **resting** heart.[4]

Blood — Interestingly, blood is one of the heaviest components of the human body, comprising about 7 percent of your total body weight. It is composed of solid particles, the blood cells, and a liquid called plasma.

Blood cells are produced by tissue found in bones, notably the ribs, spine and pelvis. An average 150-pound man's body contains five to six quarts of blood, which fulfills the circulation function linking the digestive, respiratory and excretory systems while transporting food, water and oxygen throughout the body.[5] A single blood cell completes a circuit within about one minute, travelling up to ten miles per hour.

Vascular System — As one system with the heart and transporting the body's supply of blood, the vascular system contains arteries through which oxygen-enriched (bright red) blood is pumped. Arteries are a network of ever smaller tubes that reach microscopic capillaries which nourish tissue. After yielding the oxygen and becoming darker in hue, the blood is returned to the heart through veins which are more numerous than arteries and usually larger in diameter, with thinner walls. They are equipped with valves which prevent a backflow since the blood must be forced against the pull of gravity. Otherwise the structure of veins and arteries is the same and consists of: a tough outer casing, a fibrous middle layer and the inner bore.[6]

The Lungs — Since at any given moment half your body weight is composed of oxygen and since every cell within the body must receive oxygen and remove carbon dioxide, the importance of the lungs can be adequately appreciated. They are the central element of the gas transference process called respiration, without which life could not be sustained.[7]

Muscles and Bones — These form the basis of the musculoskeletal system, housing and protecting soft parts of the body and allowing us to maintain posture. Bone consists of water, two-thirds mineral (e.g. calcium) and the remainder organic matter. They also contain blood-forming elements. Muscles are attached to bones and impart power and strength to all bodily movements. They are grouped into complementary and opposed pairs (e.g. biceps vs. triceps), each of which are further subdivided into fast-twitch and slow-twitch fibers (the literal light and dark turkey meat reflect these). Most people have a 50-50 ratio of fast- and slow-twitch fiber; fast twitch is for sprinting, slow for endurance activities (marathons as an example).[8] Remember that muscle tissue burns calories.[9]

Digestive System — This consists of the mouth, gut, esophagus, stomach, small and large intestines, liver, gall bladder and pancreas, all of which combine to aid you in the ingestion and digestion of your giant cheese and bean burrito, breaking the foods down in an intricate series of processes that supply the body with ever-simpler chemical substances for building, maintenance and energy. Like the heart and arteries, the system is subject to a dazzling array of ills and is often the place where cop-borne psychosomatic illnesses tend to appear.[10]

Liver — The body's largest internal organ is like a chemical factory: it neutralizes toxins; converts food into storageable materials; manufactures blood coagulants; stores vitamins and produces enzymes among other essential-to-life functions.[11]

Body Fat — could accurately be described as stored energy; foods (calories) that were not burned up after you ate them. A source of profound embarrassment for many millions of Americans. You know you have too much of it if little children approach you on the beach while you're sunbathing and try to drag you into the surf saying **"save yourself, Orca, swim out!"** Too much of it constitutes a **very** grave health risk. Ultimately, any food ingested can wind up being permanently stored as body fat.

Blood Fats — include **cholesterol,** a waxy-grey substance made by the liver **and eaten** as animal products: eggs, meat, cheese, milk, etc. This villain greatly contributes to occurrences of heart attacks by building up on arterial walls and blocking blood flow within the three coronary arteries.

Cholesterol — appears as either low density lipoprotein, LDL, the harmful substance that clogs your arteries; or high density lipoprotein, HDL, probably the single most important substance for naturally undoing the damage already done; this is **good** cholesterol; or VLDL, very low density lipoprotein which is **very** bad.

Triglycerides — are substances in the blood formed to facilitate fat consumption by the body; they are water soluble and make up a large portion of your VLDL's. They are not friendly.

Saturated Fats — usually solid at room temperature, lard is a good example. High consumption of this type of food increases blood cholesterol levels. Originating in milk and meat but also found in vegetable products, coconut oil, for example.

Polyunsaturated Fats —are of plant origin and tend to **lower** your levels of triglycerides and cholesterol, they are usually liquid at room temperature.

Glycogen is a storage form of glucose or blood sugar; an energy imparting system found in the liver and muscle tissues.

Adipose Tissue —where fat is stored by the body.

Insulin —is a natural hormone produced by the pancreas that facilitates the transformation of glucose and amino acids (two basic fuels of the body) into, respectively, glycogen and body protein. It also aids in the movement of these substances into other tissues, muscle, for example. And it expedites the movement of fatty acids (butter, cream, etc.) into fat cells where they are stored for future energy needs.

A few other terms you should also be familiar with:

Aerobic —in the **presence** of oxygen.

Anaerobic —in the **absence** of oxygen.

Calorie —a unit of measure—the amount of heat required to raise 1 kilogram of water 1 degree centigrade. In your body, 3,500 calories equal one pound of stored fat.

Cellulite —another word for fat; frequently appears when body fat percentage exceeds 20%.

Enzyme —an organic catalyst that speeds up chemical reactions.

Metabolism —bodily processes of energy production and utilization.

In ensuing chapters you will see and understand how the marvelous machine, the human body, is called upon to perform police work (or any work) in the face of serious nutritional deficiencies; how its physiology and health are constantly threatened by sleep deprivation, constant stress, lack of exercise and societal, family and peer group pressures.

All of these internal and environmental dangers, in addition to the serious health risks embodied by substance addictions, form an imposing array of health risks that in whole or in part combine to transform an officer into a zombie, a species of treadmill-walker who no longer enjoys much about his career or his life.

Because there are so many variables interacting: powerful genetic as well as environmental influences together, few of us are affected in the same harmful way at the same instant. What is important to understand is this: true good health like bad health is, more often than not, an **individual's choice.** Illnesses usually result from a combination of independent factors happening sequentially. To only treat the symptoms is to miss the salient point entirely; that is, to avoid, as far as possible, contact with the factors that make you ill.

Sounds simple, but so many millions of Americans choose not to do this simplest of necessities: avoid bad things, embrace good things.

You must recognize that your intellect and experience count for much in your decision to stay healthy and live a long and productive life. Most of us know the things that are bad for us, things that harm our bodies and our minds. But habit is a powerful thing, particularly when it is constantly reinforced by the bad habits of colleagues and friends.

Motivation to change life-styles in a healthy and permanent manner can obviously only come from within you: decisions that take some commitment and much courage. In most cases, the rewards are very profound and nearly immediate.

Chapter V

LIFE-STYLE DEATHS

THE THOUSAND NATURAL SHOCKS

Most police officers, as you probably know, do not meet their end in gun battles with bad guys, nor do they die as the direct result of serious job-related injuries. Like the larger U.S. population, the vast majority of cops succumb to the less-than-prosaic killers that lurk across the American landscape: heart disease, cancer, stroke and others.

Unlike the rest of American society, however, police officers who die natural deaths do so at a much younger age than do their civilian contemporaries, a somber circumstance that cuts short hard-earned retirement years, truncating in the process precious days that could have been spent with grandchildren and other loved ones.[1]

No thoughtful person would deny that life and good health constitute an individual's most precious gifts; so elemental, so essential and yet so taken for granted by millions of Americans, many of whom choose, consciously, rationally or not, to suffer bad health and to opt for an early grave.

But bad health, more often than not, is the result of individual choice. Each year, hundreds of thousands of human lives culminate in untimely deaths because of these choices.

Life-style deaths are endemic within the Western world. They are a grotesque specter of our civilization and a commentary thereon: persons literally feeding themselves to death or drinking and driving themselves there, to name only a few of the life-style manners of mortality.

These unnecessary and unfortunate patterns of behavior contribute to relegating American males, despite the fact they inhabit one of the most prosperous cultures in the world, to fortieth place among nations in life expectancy.[2]

Cops, of course, due in large part to the unrelenting demands made of them over the length of a career, fare much worse than civilians, with an

39

average life expectancy of about sixty years, thirteen years less than the general population.[3]

Can you beat the odds against long life? Yes, but not without a fundamental understanding of the things that threaten your existence.

The condition of your arteries, particularly their inner walls, exerts a profound effect on your health and longevity. At birth the arteries are supple and their inner surfaces smooth and pristine, capable of the transportation of oxygenated and nutrient-bearing blood throughout your body. As aging progresses, the effects of too many high cholesterol and other fatty foods become evident. The smooth inner surfaces become marbled by blood fats which adhere to the artery walls, diminishing the diameter through which the blood travels.

As these substances harden into plaque the arteries begin to lose their suppleness; the irregular surface that results now causes more and more fatty substances to adhere the same way dirt will adhere more easily to the already soiled surface of an automobile. The heart is forced to pump more often in order to transmit the same volume of blood through the ever-narrowing channels. Untreated, this condition, called arteriosclerosis or hardening of the arteries, is a major cause of death in the United States, particularly when the blockage occurs within the three coronary arteries which supply blood to the heart muscle itself.

A study conducted during the Korean War disclosed the effects of the typical American diet on the coronary arteries. Autopsies were performed on many American, Chinese and Korean soldiers killed in combat. Thirty-five percent of the Americans already displayed significant narrowing of their arteries, even though the average age of these men was only twenty-two. Follow-up studies revealed similar findings among young American soldiers killed in Vietnam. Examinations conducted on Asians, Japanese males aged 20–30, indicated no artery narrowing whatsoever.[4]

Diet was and is the difference; an American diet, loaded with fatty foods: cheeseburgers, bacon and eggs, milk shakes, donuts and so on, versus the Asians' diet, largely composed of fish and complex carbohydrates, rice and other vegetables.

As the diameter of the arteries diminishes due to fat buildup, blood pressure often becomes elevated to compensate, exerting more wear and tear both on the heart and the thickened and increasingly brittle artery walls. This pressure applied unceasingly to the already damaged arterial tissue results in more damage. Weak points begin to develop which threaten the entire arterial subsystem and not just those arteries adjacent to the heart but throughout the body, including the brain.[5]

High blood pressure (hypertension) usually produces no noticeable symptoms. Because of this fact, it is called the silent killer. Many persons with the affliction are unaware of their condition.[6] The causes of hypertension are little known, though heredity plays an important role. Besides damaging and thickening the artery walls, high blood pressure greatly increases the risk both of heart attack and stroke. Generally speaking, life expectancy is greatest when blood pressure lies between 100/60 and 130/80.[7] Beyond the latter figure, life expectancy is progressively shortened as blood pressure increases. About 58 million people in the U.S. are afflicted. Blacks are inordinately affected: 38% have high blood pressure.[8] It is the leading cause of death among black Americans.

Among the female population, women using oral contraceptives and those past the age of menopause are disproportionately affected. And, perhaps predictably, high blood pressure's effects become more manifest with advancing age. Besides heredity, obesity greatly increases your risk of hypertension.[9]

When arteriosclerosis and high blood pressure interact they create a particularly deadly duality. But whether occurring in conjunction or singularly these two are prolific killers responsible for many thousands of deaths annually; both are horrifically well represented among the ten leading causes of death in the United States.

Even a cursory examination of the list of leading killers in this country lends strong credence to the concept of life-style deaths, since all, wholly or in part, can be attributed to tragic, often lifelong decisions made by individuals. What follows is a summarization and discussion of each of the leading causes of death in the United States. Statistics furnished by the U.S. Department of Health and Human Services for 1989.

Heart Disease: long the leading cause of death in the U.S. though declining in numbers since the early seventies (perhaps the result of healthier dietary practices and improved medical care), heart attacks, including all cases diagnosed as ischemic heart disease, still claimed over 740,000 lives yearly. These deaths are exclusive of those from angina pectoris and other coronary diseases. In medical terminology heart attack is myocardial infarction or death of the heart muscle.[10] The same condition may also be referred to as **coronary thrombosis**, which describes a blood clot within a coronary artery. These conditions can occur in conjunction or singularly.

Arteriosclerosis aggravates and can lead to coronary thrombosis by narrowing the inner diameter of the coronary arteries which supply blood to the heart. The normal channels of these arteries are only one-eighth inch in diameter to begin with; narrowed by disease they are much more likely to become completely blocked by a clot.

Though there's no way to predict a heart attack with precision, many heart attack survivors often recall vague pains, breathlessness or fatigue for days preceding the attack. Indeed, many victims actually sought medical attention in the days or weeks before the attack occurred.[11]

Pain associated with actual occurrence is felt usually in the left arm/shoulder, accompanied by sweating, nausea and loss of consciousness. Some authorities on the subject indicate that one-half of all first heart attack victims perish, including about 15 to 20% who do not survive the first five days following an attack.[12]

Prolonged stress or an acute period of stress can trigger an attack: any event that necessitates more work demanded of the heart than blood flow that can be delivered to support the effort, or the presence of a clot cutting off blood supply to the heart. This crisis is the culmination of a slow, silent process, often of many years' duration.

Factors which increase the risk of heart attack include age, smoking, family history, diabetes, lack of exercise, personality type, sex, blood pressure and weight. Though women are generally less prone than men to suffer heart attack, use of oral contraceptives has been demonstrated to increase their risk. A female who smokes and uses oral contraceptives is two to three times more likely to experience an attack compared to a woman who neither smokes nor uses oral contraceptives.[13]

Persons at high risk would do well to regularly have analyzed their blood cholesterol levels. An average cholesterol level in the U.S. is 220 (measured in milligrams/deciliter), but a number of medical authorities advise that a safe level is below 200.[14] (Note: a definitive understanding of the impact of HDL cholesterol will be discussed in a later chapter.)

Some heart attack victims exhibit a form of denial even in the face of unmistakable symptoms. Though this behavior may be motivated by fear, anger or even embarrassment, it is critical that medical attention be immediately sought. Don't ignore symptoms that feel like indigestion, for example, when the discomfort persists for hours or even days. Studies indicate that most patients delay seeking treatment for three hours after symptoms occur, longer if they occur during the nighttime.[15] Early warning signs of potential impending attack most noticeable include angina pectoris, a sharp pain in the chest caused by a temporary interruption in the blood supply due to stress or exertion.[16]

According to the Framingham Report on Coronary Disease, about half of all heart attacks take place between eleven at night and six in the morning. Additionally, the report concluded, a heavy meal, eaten before going to bed, obviously heightens the risk: introducing a high concentration of blood fats to be metabolized precisely when the body is slowing down and least able to dispose of fats properly. This condition can cause a clot to form which causes the attack.[17] Small meals before retiring to bed should be the rule, **regardless** of what time of the day or night you sleep.

Though coronary bypasses have become a multi-billion dollar industry in this country, the procedure only treats the **symptoms** and not the causes. In the absence of changed, healthier dietary practices, the new grafts clog up much faster than the original artery, often necessitating a future operation within five years.[18] And, of course, there's a limit to the number of times this surgical technique can be administered. At best, a bypass operation buys you time to change your habits.

Finally, it must be emphasized that, among professional groups, police officers are highly prone to experience heart attacks. In a survey of 149 professional occupations, cops ranked tenth highest, ahead of doctors, lawyers and professors.[19]

Cancer: the second leading cause of death among Americans. It claimed nearly 495,000 lives in 1989 despite the fact that great strides have been made in cancer treatment. Yet, 60% of those contracting cancer still succumb to the disease. The causes of cancer are many and varied, since cancer is actually more than one hundred different diseases possessing a common characteristic: the abnormal growth, division and proliferation of cells spreading from site of origin to other parts of the body.[20] As they spread these cells invade and destroy normal organs and tissues. Approximately 800,000 new cases of cancer appear each year, exclusive of about 400,000 annual cases of skin cancer which is usually caused by prolonged exposure to the sun and can be fatal.[21]

Various life-style choices can provoke the origination and proliferation of cancer cells. **Any condition which depresses the effectiveness of the body's immune system can contribute.** Prolonged stress, poor nutrition, diets high in fat and low in fiber, even obesity appear to create an increased vulnerability. Persons in poor physical condition run an added risk as do those coming into contact with various chemicals: asbestos, benzene, vinyl chloride, to name a few. Even excessive and prolonged exposure to x-rays can induce cancerous cells to originate.[22]

A significant proportion of cancers can be prevented through life-style choices. Smoking is the leading cause of lung cancer deaths which claimed 139,000 lives in 1989. An increase in the number of women who smoke has resulted in increasingly more deaths among females from this type. Lung cancer is the number one killer of males among cancer deaths and has edged breast cancer as the leading cause of cancer deaths in women.[23]

The progression of cancer cell location occurs in three stages:

1. **Localized** — limited to its original site.
2. **Regional** — reaching into adjacent organs or lymph nodes.
3. **Distant** — carried into other parts of the body.[24]

For every type of cancer, the prognosis is much better if the cancerous tissue is localized relatively early in the progression of the disease. For that reason, early detection is a vital variable in survival. The longer the disease has to spread, the less favorable the outlook for recovery. Breast cancer, as an example, has a survival rate above 80% if discovered still in the localized stage. If discovered in the regional phase, the survival rate slips to about 55% and in the distant stage decreases to between 1 to 22%, depending on the site of origination.[25]

In the face of such factors, complete annual medical examinations, especially past the age of 40, become an intelligent and wise life-style decision. In addition, women should learn and practice self breast examination at least monthly, and all should be alert to the warning signs that may indicate the presence of the disease, practicing, in essence, an awareness of the body and any changes that could be significant. Several warning signals listed by the American Cancer Society are:

- Change in bowel or bladder habits.
- A sore that does not heal.
- Unusual bleeding or discharge.
- Thickening or lump in breast or elsewhere.
- Indigestion or difficulty in swallowing.
- Obvious change in a wart or mole.
- Nagging cough or hoarseness.

It should also be remembered that even though cancer can strike at any age, the risk of contracting the disease increases with advancing age.[26]

Stroke: the third most common cause of death; cerebrovascular diseases claimed over 146,000 lives. Strokes occur within the human brain, the result either of blockage within an artery (or much less commonly a vein) or by the rupture of a cerebral blood vessel. Medically these injuries are classified:

Cerebral Hemorrhage: Rupture of an artery or vein which causes bleeding into the brain.

Cerebral Thrombosis: Caused by an obstruction of a cerebral blood vessel when a blood clot forms within the blood vessel's walls. Can be due to abnormal thickening of the blood; damage to the wall from arteriosclerosis or atherosclerosis (fatty deposits) or inflammation of the vessels.

Cerebral Embolism: An obstruction caused by a blood clot or other foreign matter which has migrated from another part of the body. Commonly disables the side of the brain that supplies speech and movement to the body's right side.

Additionally, an Aneurysm: A defect in the substance of the arteries present at birth, can stretch, enlarge, rupture and bleed into the membrane that covers the brain.[27]

The human brain needs about 20% of the body's total blood supply in order to function. Interruption in this supply will cause unconsciousness within ten to twelve seconds. If the blood supply is stopped or reduced below one-fourth of its normal level, cerebral infarction ensues, a condition which results in permanent brain damage.[28]

It is important to note that various physical conditions greatly increase the risk of stroke. These include high blood pressure, diabetes, elevated blood fats, heart disease, obesity and smoking. Early diagnosis and treatment of these conditions is an important first step in the prevention of strokes. The peak incidence of stroke is attained usually about age 50 and continues through 70 years.[29] Because people age at varying rates, however, mere chronological age cannot alone indicate your susceptibility since physical age can differ greatly among individuals. Physical age, when lower than chronological age, often represents a victory of healthy life-styles, which acts to slow the degrading effects of the passing years. Men have a higher incidence of strokes in the earlier decades than women probably due to the protective effect provided by female hormones. Past menopause, however, females tend to catch up with males in the occurrences of stroke.[30]

Fortunately, there are warning signs which can precede a major stroke:

Transient Ischemic Attack (TIA)—like angina pectoris, caused by a temporary interruption of the blood supply. Short in duration they normally result in complete recovery.
Reversible Ischemic Neurological Deficits (RINDS)—relatively small infarctions (softening of the brain); usually complete or nearly complete recovery results.

Recognition of TIA and RINDS is vital; proper medical treatment can prevent a future major stroke.[31]

Though the incidence of stroke is decreasing, mortality figures are still replete with tens of thousands of unnecessary deaths each year. Further, non-fatal major strokes are the most common disabler of Americans: more than two million individuals have suffered disability due to this affliction.[32] And finally, the most viable defense remains a healthy amount of moderation in life-style decisions.

Accidents: the fourth leading cause of death. Accidents accounted for over 92,000 lives. They are the leading cause of death among persons under 35 years of age. Motor vehicle accidents accounted for more than 47,000 of these. Again, life-style decisions impacted heavily: the use of alcohol was involved in over half all fatal accidents, not just motor vehicles but drownings, fires, suffocations, firearms, and poisonings, as well.[33]

Obstructive Pulmonary Diseases/Emphysema: the fifth leading cause accounting for over 83,000 deaths. The obstructive pulmonary diseases include bronchitis, asthma and emphysema. Both chronic bronchitis and emphysema usually occur in conjunction and are largely caused by smoking, though other environmental substances can cause or irritate bronchitis.

Emphysema is a condition in which the air sacs in the lung become enlarged, dilated and inelastic. The disease kills by slowly smothering its victim. Symptoms include shortness of breath, wheezing, chronic coughing and the expectoration of bitter sputum. It is an increasingly common disease that strikes many more men than women, particularly men between the ages of 50 and 70. Like other obstructive lung diseases, emphysema is characterized by greatly enlarged lungs. There is no successful treatment for emphysema: its effects are irreversible.[34]

Pneumonia (and Influenza): this sixth leading cause is primarily a disease of the elderly and resulted in over 75,000 deaths. Pneumonia is any infection of the air spaces of the lung whether bacterial or viral in origin. Often viral pneumonia appears as a complication of the late stages of other diseases such as cancer or heart disease.

Those persons who are normally healthy experience a relatively mild illness and can usually recover without seeking medical attention. Chronic stress, poor nutrition and inadequate rest can all interact to make an individual more susceptible.[35]

Viral pneumonia is caused by many types of virus, but the most common is the influenza virus. Symptoms include stuffy nose, watery eyes, muscle aches and headaches, fever and severe fatigue.[36]

Influenza occurs both in periodic worldwide epidemics and isolated local outbreaks usually during winter months. Available vaccine is especially important for the elderly and the chronically ill in whom the flu produces the most severe disease and complications.[37]

Diabetes: this disease usually kills its victim through its complications, notably premature hardening of the arteries, strokes, heart attacks and kidney disease. More than 46,000 deaths were attributed to this affliction. Five percent of the American population has diabetes.[38]

The major characteristic of the disease is the body's inability to regulate glucose (sugar) in the blood. The disease occurs in two types:

> **Juvenile Diabetes** — 15% of all diabetics have this type. These individuals usually develop the disease as children or young adults and are usually thin. Their bodies have a total or nearly total lack of insulin which is a hormone essential in maintaining sugar levels in the blood. These patients usually need daily injections of the hormone.
> **Adult-Onset Diabetes** — affects older persons, usually those past the age of 40 who are overweight. In many cases weight reduction alone will result in improving the condition or eliminating it. Insulin injections are usually not necessary, but the adult-onset diabetic is at risk to develop life-threatening complications.[39]

These complications become more serious as the diabetic ages. He or she is seventeen times more likely to suffer kidney disease and twenty-five times more likely to become blind, and about 5 percent of all diabetics suffer permanent blindness.[40]

Men and women are equally likely to be affected by the disease, with highest incidence occurring between ages 40 to 60.

Symptoms of adult-onset diabetes include chronic fatigue and thirst, frequent urination and increased appetite. Some patients develop numbness or tingling in the extremities and blurred vision.

Advanced symptoms which usually occur with age include slow healing wounds and the very real danger of developing gangrene with resultant necessity for amputation of toes and feet. Prompt diagnosis and lifelong treatment do minimize the risk of complications. The adult-onset disease is common, easy to diagnose and treat and can be .controlled by making life-style decisions affecting proper nutrition and exercise. Adult diabetes need not ever become life-threatening.[41]

Suicide: claimed almost 30,000 lives and, as you know, is probably underreported, possibly by as much as half. Perennially it is a leading cause of death in the U.S. and the obvious end of the spectrum when life-style decisions are considered.

Chronic Liver Disease and Cirrhosis: heavy and prolonged abuse of alcohol is the most common cause of severe liver injury in the United States, though there are many other causes of the affliction not related to alcohol. Cirrhosis is a progressive disease that slowly destroys liver tissue and contributed to well over 26,000 deaths as a leading cause of mortality. Death follows liver failure and internal hemorrhaging.

The initial stage of cirrhosis is the fatty liver during which the liver becomes enlarged, its cells fat engorged, and it takes on a pale hue. This change produces no symptoms and few laboratory abnormalities. Continued heavy drinking results in the inflammation of organ tissue and death of some lower cells. At this point abstinence from alcohol **can** result in reversal of the injuries. Cirrhosis is the fastest-growing killer of adults aged 25 to 64.[42]

Atherosclerosis: a form of arteriosclerosis in which the membranes lining one or more arteries become thickened after which cholesterol and other fats build up, reducing or obstructing blood flow. Over 19,000 persons died from the effects of atherosclerosis. High blood fats obviously cause and worsen the condition as do family history, smoking, high blood pressure, obesity, diabetes, physical inactivity and emotional stress. The rate of diagnosis is most frequent between the ages of 45 and 55, though it is not rare in patients under 40. Similar increases are noted in women due to use of the contraceptive pill.[43]

As you no doubt noticed, there are recurring factors that increase your susceptibility to a number of these killers. Obesity, lack of physical activity, prolonged stress, cigarettes and elevated blood fats contribute, sometimes alone, more often in conjunction, to undermine and degrade your health and raise the risks you run of an early death. Some of these factors, in turn, interact to produce diabetes, a prime contributor to the formation of more serious conditions.

Taken as an illuminating and cumulative cause and effect, consider this: ingested cholesterol and saturated fats and a chronic lack of physical activity has probably killed more Americans than were killed in all our wars and all our traffic accidents combined. Indisputably these factors have resulted in millions upon millions of unnecessary deaths from the dawn of our evolution into a modern industrialized society, until now. And cholesterol is a legal substance!

The very concept of life-style deaths presupposes the existence of life-style choice. More and more frequently, Americans by the tens of millions are opting to take charge of their individual destinies through mature decisions and moderation in all things. Unfortunately, for the 1.6 million Americans about whom you just read, their days for decisions are past, eternally.

Chapter VI

NUTRITION

On the subject of nutrition and food there is evident a paradox: that which nourishes and sustains life can also kill you. Somewhere between these extremes each of us must discover his or her middle ground in order to achieve true health and fitness. There are no exceptions to this rule: if you practice unhealthy eating habits you cannot hope to be healthy, no matter how frequently or how hard you exercise.

The harmful effects of improper eating can be very evident: a bulging waistline, for example. Or they can be invisible to even a trained observer: partially blocked coronary arteries, their walls caked with hardened plaque which facilitates the continuing buildup of fatty deposits.

Obviously, your eating behavior is learned, beginning in earliest childhood. As an elemental motivation performed throughout life, three or more times a day, these habits are powerfully ingrained and cannot be changed without a determined, unceasing effort. First, however, you've got to fully understand the complex interplay of food types within your body. To say the least, nutrition is a fertile field of study considering the hundreds of books that have been published on the subject, including those that deal solely with the numerous ways to diet, or limiting the intake and controlling the types of food ingested.

I do not believe in dieting to lose or maintain your body weight, particularly since I know people who have **dieted** for ten, even as long as fifteen years without **permanently** attaining their goals. So the word diet when used in this chapter merely refers to the sum total of all the foods you eat; it does not mean starving yourself to lose weight.

This fertile productive land of ours produces far more food than we, as a nation, can hope to consume. And yet this very monument to our prosperity tends to contribute to our bad eating habits. Food is everywhere. It is plentiful, it is convenient and it is cheap. There are no shortages of food in America so we are free to select from a vast assortment of foods, often exercising the ingrained and immature eating habits of small children as we do so.

Despite the obvious facts that food represents a vital life-sustaining substance and that its effects on each of us are present every minute of our lives, having significant impact not only upon our physical but our behavioral selves, our society exhibits abysmal ignorance of this most important subject. Indeed, even physicians tend to ignore the significant effects food can contribute to poor health unless it has been diagnosed as a primary cause of disease, in a case such as botulism, for example. Think about it. When was the last time your physician asked you what you ate each day?[1]

If the patterns of your existence, all factors: physical, psychological and environmental, were weaved together into a tapestry, food would be the dominant color so much does it effect who you are, what you are and how you are.

As in many things, a little fundamental knowledge can go far to dispel the distortions, myths and inaccuracies commonly held concerning this important subject. And so, to the facts.

An investigator assigned to look into a case of obesity which resulted in sudden death, who continually comes across references to **calories**, might, in time, be prompted to conclude that too many calories in fact did the victim in. Would he be right in his assumption? Well, yes and no.

Strictly speaking, a calorie is only a unit of measurement; the amount of heat necessary to raise the temperature of one kilogram of water, one degree centigrade. Obviously this is a pretty abstract bit of information, not really applicable to much in our day-to-day lives. When you think of it as measuring a minute amount of energy, however, the term takes on significance. If food is energy and stored body fat is unburned energy, the calorie serves as an indicator of what's being burned vs. what's not. Thirty-five hundred calories stored around your waist equate to one pound of utter uselessness.[2]

All the foods we eat are divided into three sources:

Fats — the most concentrated form of energy from food — contain more than twice as many calories as equal portions of either carbohydrates or protein. Chief sources include salad and cooking oils, meat, poultry, butter, eggs, and other dairy products, to name a few. Nine calories per gram.

Protein — found in ample supply both in plant and animal sources and consisting of nine essential amino acids; once believed to be an abundant source of energy, an assumption since proven inaccurate.[3] Protein is vital for the growth, maintenance and repair of bodily tissue. Four calories per gram.

Carbohydrates — among the most common foods, these are derived mainly from plants and are composed of sugars and starches. They are primarily energy-imparting substances. Four calories per gram.

Each of these food sources is essential to good nutritional health. The problems arise on a standard American diet which consists of twice as much protein and fat as the human body needs. The composition of that diet looks like:

43% Protein   37% Fats   20% Carbohydrates[4]

Such an intake contains too many unnecessary calories from fats and twice as much protein as is necessary to maintain the body. The excesses over the body's needs are stored as unburned energy (that's the lump around your middle) or, just as dangerously, become blood fats that adhere to your arterial walls limiting the volume of blood that can be transported and making your heart work much harder than it needs to. So, calories as a function of excessive food intake did indeed contribute to doing in our obese sudden-death victim.

And yet, caloric intake alone cannot completely explain obesity or related health problems. Because you are a unique individual working a particularly demanding job at all hours of the night and day, your nutritional life-style must be scrutinized on an individual basis in order to accurately and adequately understand how your eating habits affect your health. These factors include shift work, the number, types and times of meals consumed per day, the amount of real sleep you experience within twenty-four hours and the amount of regular exercise in which you partake; this is assuming you do not suffer from gastrointestinal or other ills which tend to limit your choices of foods.

An old maxim says "eat breakfast like a king, lunch like a prince and dinner like a pauper." Adapted for cops we know that shift work tends to confuse your body's metabolism both leading to (and stemming from) sleep deprivation and related gastrointestinal problems which are further aggravated by other stressors common to the profession.

For the purposes of this immediate discussion let's dispense with the generic names for mealtimes: breakfast, lunch and dinner, replacing them with the time of day you eat.

When working rotating shifts you can maintain your body weight or reduce it on an average caloric intake (an average 2,200 for men and 1,600 for women: a more precise computation follows) by consuming your largest meal before you leave home for work. This is based on the assumption that your calorie burn per hour is greatest while you are working. Studies have demonstrated that large meals consumed before bedtime cause you to gain weight over months; conversely, a large meal ingested before the work day begins negates the tendency to store fat because the calories are burned through both physical (infrequent for cops) and mental exertion. The large pre-work meal is then supplemented for the remainder of the 24-hour day by two small meals, each about 25 percent of your caloric intake: one while at work and the third after you've returned home and well before you go to bed.[5]

A further complication arises as you enter middle age. At that point (at whatever age you attain it) your metabolism begins to slow; the relative calmness that usually comes with advancing age and your body needs fewer calories.[6]

It is often at this point in their lives when people who've been trim for a lifetime begin to experience middle-age spread even though they haven't altered their eating habits. To counterbalance this condition, they are advised to consume 80 percent of their calories before one in the afternoon; to keep as active as possible and to reduce their total caloric intake, since their body no longer needs as much fuel as it did in their earlier years.

This is fine for retired persons or those working only daywork. But shift work again compounds the problem. So, continue to eat your biggest meal, 35–50 percent of total calories before you leave for work.[7] Then the meal you consume while at work should round your caloric intake (to that point in your 24-hour eating cycle) to 80 percent with the remaining meal consumed sometime after you get off. This regimen will assist you in maintaining your body weight with exercise, or slightly reducing it.

An additional problem arises, particularly on the midnight shift when you have two or three (or more) consecutive days off. During that interval you are expected to resume regular eating patterns, though a few days is usually not enough to acclimate your body to normal mealtimes.

My advice is to eat three or four or more **light** meals during each of your days off, with 80 percent consumed before 1:00 p.m.; these small meals punish your digestive system less than heavier meals, interfere less with your resumption (or attempted resumption) of normal sleeping times and continue to contribute to your desired level of weight maintenance.

Obviously, what you eat has as much significance as when you eat it. The American trait of eating one's self into the grave has evolved over many years. Yes, part of it is a result of our incredible agricultural productivity, unprecedented in world history. Another major contributing factor involves technology: machines have obviated the need for Western mankind to perform hard manual labor. Each of subsequent generations in this century have been a little more sedentary than their parents. Also, restaurants and fast-food establishments are gradually taking a greater percentage of a family's food budget dollars. After all, fast food is satisfying, cheap and its convenience efficiently caters to the frenetic life-styles of many millions of Americans.

Within the last three generations there is another factor at work. The post-war baby boomers were, in the main, raised by parents who grew up during the Great Depression, the particularly hard days which preceded World War II and a time when animal protein was considered a luxury and a twice-a-week luxury at that. Rich fatty foods, ice cream, milk shakes, etc., which today's young people take for granted, were unknown to millions of American children growing up during the 1930s.

By the end of World War II these Depression-era children were themselves grown and beginning their own families as America entered an era of incomparable prosperity. Protein and rich fatty foods were abundant and affordable and the children of the Depression began to lavish on **their** children, the first of the Baby Boom, the foods they themselves had been deprived of. Protein from animal tissue was known to be a "good" food source. The new affluence made possible serving this "good" food at every mealtime.

And so it was done. Followed after dinner, of course, by dessert, often the richer the better. My generation, to say the obvious, did not want for adequate caloric intake nor for a wide variety of fatty foods. The predictable result: tens of millions of chronically overweight men and women and deaths from heart attacks skyrocketing.

What these parents did they did out of love and ignorance and out of an understandable parents' desire to make things better for their children. Little was known at that time about the potential bad effects of too much protein or too many fatty foods in the diet. Milk and eggs, steak and bacon, cheese and hamburgers became the core dietary elements of millions of Americans, habits retained as my generation entered adulthood, with tragic results. And not only for them, because ingrained eating habits are passed on to the following generation: today's innocent children (and grandchildren) and so the poor eating habit cycle continues but with a twist.

Today we **know** better and a child fed a steady diet of rich fatty foods together with too much protein and too many total calories is an abused child, **if** the parents know the dangers inherent to such a diet. Can you do to little ones who trust you what was done to you in ignorance? Or should you rather habituate them to healthy foods while they're young?

FATS AND FAST FOODS

At any rate, intimately attuned to America's evolved dietary preferences, the fast-food industry panders to the supposed wants and industry-perceived nutritional needs of our society.

Several years ago when I first became concerned about what I was eating, I began limiting my fast-food order to a fish sandwich; fish was supposed to be a healthy food to eat, right? Sometime later I read an article that informed me that all foods prepared in fast-food places by deep frying were prepared in beef tallow.[8] This imparts a beefy flavor to the foods which, according to industry taste-testing results, we Americans are supposed to love. So your favorite, french fries, for example, were prepared in a medium loaded with cholesterol (though in many fast-food establishments this is no longer the case). My fish sandwich probably contained as much cholesterol as a cheeseburger.

Now cholesterol, as you probably already know, has been identified as the prime contributing villain in both coronary heart disease and arteriosclerosis (hardening of the arteries). It is a waxy grey substance produced by the liver: that's right, your body produces cholesterol and it is also ingested **only** from foods provided by animal sources: milk, eggs, meat, butter, etc. Cholesterol fulfills a need within the human body. It is found in almost all cell tissues and plays a role in the digestion of fats and is also needed in the synthesis of certain hormones. Eating foods high in cholesterol raises the levels of that substance in your blood.

Americans, not surprisingly, have higher levels of cholesterol than people in other nations, especially Orientals. Too much of the stuff appears to act the way sludge behaves in a pipe: it clogs your vascular system.

There is some debate about what is an optimum amount of cholesterol for an average individual's daily intake. I say err, if you must, on the safe side and eat no more than fifty milligrams of it per day. That's comparable to five pats of butter. It's been demonstrated that limiting one's daily intake of cholesterol and exercising aerobically lowers the levels found in an individual's blood (I am living proof that it works); less in the blood equals less to block your arteries, thus reducing the risk of heart attack.[9] Ergo, it makes a lot of sense to lower your intake. An egg yolk, by the way, can contain 250 milligrams of cholesterol, five times what you should have in a whole day!

Now I'm aware of the fact that the nature of your job, particularly the uniformed patrol function, makes it very attractive to eat fast-food meals between calls for service, for example, or during a particularly busy shift. And yes, it is probably better to grab a hamburger than to skip the meal altogether, since missing a meal contributes potentially to further gastrointestinal woes.

And, to be fair, some of the fast-food chains are catching on to new health-conscious dietary trends exhibited by the American public: several offer salads now and some are advertising the fact that they use vegetable oils in some food preparation. This is an encouraging trend, showing as it does that the intelligence of American consumers can affect the variety and healthfulness of foods made available.

Though be aware, all vegetable oils are not created equal. Not originating from an animal source, they indeed contain no cholesterol. Certain types, however, are extremely high in saturated fats, substances as harmful as the cholesterol which they purport to improve upon by replacing.

Among the less healthful vegetable oils are palm and coconut.[10] These are not what you want to eat; they're harmful. Also, if you see the words **hydrogenated** or **partially hydrogenated** appearing on a package and preceding the type of oil, it's also something you'd rather avoid eating because it's also high in saturated fats.[11]

Returning to the fast-food lunch or dinner, know that a typical order: cheeseburger, french fries and a milk shake contains 78 milligrams of cholesterol.[12] That represents about 150% of your daily cholesterol allowance, and that's only one meal. It's also good to keep in mind that for every 1% reduction in your blood cholesterol, you experience a 2% reduced risk of a heart attack.[13]

Nathan Pritiken, in his book **The Pritiken Promise**, explained some additional disadvantages caused by a diet high in cholesterol and other fats. After ingesting a fatty meal, your blood is literally greasy for a number of hours. The red blood cells carry oxygen to all the tissue within your body and because these cells are coated with fatty substances they adhere to each other. At various extremities within the human body the capillaries which admit blood are only wide enough to admit the passage of red blood cells in single file. Obviously, the clumped-together cells cannot gain entrance and the contiguous tissue fed by these capillaries becomes oxygen-deprived.

That pleasant drowsy feeling you get after a delicious plate of fried chicken, then, is the direct result of oxygen deprivation within your brain and other extremities.[14] So, if you're experiencing chronic fatigue, maybe you should monitor your fat food intake more closely. This same condition also contributes to slowing your reaction time; not a real good state for a cop to put himself in. Women on high-fat diets reap an additional negative: a tendency to experience increased flow during menstrual periods; also the length of the period is increased as are the amount and severity of cramping experienced.[15]

And don't think a food has to be dripping to be high in fat content. Potato chips and similar snacks, donuts and other pastries prepared by deep frying all have a high-fat content, as do most luncheon meats and cold cuts. Most surprising to me was the fact that soup; yes, Mom's favorite cure-for-what-ails-you chicken soup, of all things, or any soup prepared using animal stock and/or marrow, is loaded with cholesterol. This is especially bad news for dieters: soup is often one of the chronic dieter's staples.

If you need proof, buy a cup from a restaurant, take it home and put it in the refrigerator overnight. In the morning you'll see a half an inch of fat congealed on the top. Skim that off and you have de-fatted soup. **Now** it's healthy.

It should be evident that fast food, because of its inordinately high fat content, does nothing so much as slow you down. Foods high in fats, though they may appear to be a dollar and nutritional bargain, are, when consumed day after day, a time bomb ticking away inside your body: adding pounds, sludging arteries, making you feel tired all the time. If you must, on occasion, eat fast foods, order a simple hamburger and side it with a salad and ice water.

PROTEIN

Animal protein was once regarded as almost a miracle food: imparting energy and at the same time facilitating muscular development. Americans eat about twice as much protein as they need to, because it's so available and relatively inexpensive.[16] Here again, habit has replaced reasonable nutritional needs.

Muscles grow larger by being stressed to exhaustion (within a carefully controlled exercise environment) in the presence of a regularly followed balanced diet.[17] More protein alone will not produce more muscle mass; the excess protein you eat simply turns to fat. And too much protein can definitely make you sick.[18]

Here's how. In the absence of enough energy-imparting carbohydrates in your diet, protein is converted to energy in a **dirty** chemical process, one of the by-products of which is ammonia, a poisonous substance that, additionally, is difficult for the body to excrete. As two ammonia molecules unite, they form urea, less toxic but still harmful to living tissue. This remaining toxicity must still be diluted, so large amounts of water from the body are required before excretion can take place without harming the kidneys. Thus, high protein diets, as Pritiken noted, are extremely dehydrating.[19]

This phenomenon has special significance for older people. As we age many of us will actually lose our thirst sensation. Add to the habit of rarely drinking water with an already dehydrating high protein diet and you've created a potentially life-threatening situation, particularly if an individual must exert himself under a blistering summer sun (like cops occasionally have to do). This condition comes to light around the country when an elderly person is brought to a hospital emergency room disoriented, often hardly able to speak, but recovers immediately when simply given liquid to ingest.[20]

There is also evidence to suggest that high protein diets contribute to the condition called osteoporosis by depleting calcium, a major cause of weakening and thinning of the bones.[21] All of us have known elderly persons to whom an accidental bump against a piece of furniture, a collision that wouldn't even bruise a healthy adult, results in a fractured hip. Brittle, weakened bone tissue, loss of height and posture and premature aging are all the symptoms of this terrible progressive and degenerative disease, one that's much more frequently suffered by women than men.

Protein also reduces your capacity to engage in endurance activities. Tests have shown that athletes on high-protein diets are consistently outperformed **by a margin of three to one** by athletes on complex carbohydrate diets.[22]

And, finally, remember protein is still the most expensive form of food. Pritiken estimated that a family of four, minimizing their animal protein intake, could save more than $1,500 a year in grocery bills.[23] The equivalent of four ounces of baked chicken each day is all the protein you will ever need!

CARBOHYDRATES

These foods are the grains and the grasses, a primary source of nutrition for mankind since time immemorial, but a source in disfavor among millions of Americans for various reasons. Natural foods, whole wheat bread, for example, actually have to be chewed before they can be swallowed, not like white bread made with bleached white flour that saves you so many valuable minutes you might have had to spend chewing. Then too, rice, for example — "**that's what all those foreigners eat; it's not real American food like a hot dog or a steak.**"

Also you've probably at some time in your life (having gained a few pounds) been told by a physician to "lay off" the fattening foods, "no spaghetti, cut back on the bread and potatoes and absolutely no pizza or anything like that." Ever heard that from a doctor? I know plenty of people who have and who, in consequence, rejected the very foods that would have greatly helped them lose, then maintain, their weight.

Now, I don't claim to be a doctor (some of my favorite people are doctors), but, for the fun of it, next time you visit yours ask him or her how many courses in nutrition they had in medical school. At most you'll probably hear "one," but the more frequent response will be **none.** That's because courses on nutrition were rarely offered in many schools of medicine in the past! So a doctor telling you to lay off bread in order to trim your waistline is speaking, nutritionally, as a layman.[24]

Remember, carbohydrates have only four calories per gram versus nine calories per gram of fat. And carbohydrates give you energy and endurance; they also burn at an average rate of two calories per minute; you don't get physical peaks and valleys roller coastering your metabolism.

And where a chemical by-product of protein is a poison, ammonia, the only chemical by-products resulting from carbohydrates are natural:

carbon dioxide and water, neither of which is poisonous and both of which are easily and safely excreted by the body.

Pasta, in all its delicious variations is a complex carbohydrate that's cheap, easily digested and an excellent nutritional source of energy. The potato, like spaghetti, often maligned as a fattening food, is a marvel of nutritional value, containing as much protein as a slice of bacon, as much fiber as a tossed salad and is an excellent natural source of vitamins C and B6; all for only 100–150 calories. It wasn't the baked potato that was fattening, it was the sour cream or butter.

Studies continue to confirm: cultures which consume a large percentage of their diets in the form of complex carbohydrates have consistently much lower incidences of coronary heart disease.[25] Some types of complex carbohydrates actually lower the presence of cholesterol in your blood, particularly its harmful component, LDL.

Additionally, a diet that includes vegetables, fruits and grains has been shown to decrease the risk of colon-rectal cancer; these same fibrous foods prevent constipation and other painful colon problems including irritable bowel syndrome and colitis (both often associated with the type A personality: overachievers in uniform); and in some cases addition of fiber to one's diet has been found to be instrumental in controlling blood sugar in mild cases of diabetes.[26]

Complex Carbohydrates, if they sound like miracle food, they are. The sad irony is these most basic foods have been around for thousands of years and our prosperous culture chose (and largely still chooses) to ignore them. I wonder how many hundreds of thousands of deaths could have been prevented in this country simply by a change in diet. Complex carbohydrates: beans, peas, pasta, rice, oatmeal, buckwheat pancakes, whole wheat breads, apples, pears, bananas, grapes and so on should constitute more than 70% of all the foods you eat every day of your life.[27] They represent a conscious decision made by you to maintain health and optimum weight; in societies where these foods constitute 80 percent or more of the diet, the incidence of obesity approaches zero.

Complex carbohydrates can help keep you muscular and trim.

WATER

While water is not a nutrient, it is an extremely important bodily need, another inexpensive, universally available source of good health that is largely ignored. When I've told cops they should drink more water I got, "**you mean in my scotch?**" "**No,**" I'd say, "**water that comes from the tap. You know, from a sink, like in your kitchen?**" More blank looks, "**What does he mean?**" they would say.

It sounds elementary, but about 65% of your body is composed of water. In fact, take away the water from a 200-pound man and he would weigh 60 pounds. There are four major systems in the body that use large quantities of water:

• The lungs use about 2 glasses per day.
• The skin loses about the same through respiration and perspiration.
• The kidneys use about 5 to 6 glasses per day.
• The intestines which lose about one-half glass per day.[28]

This totals ten or so glasses per day. You should know that your body manufactures some water and also derives water from foods taken in. Water removes toxins, mucus and sludge from your body; it propels waste materials out; lubricates your moving body parts and increases blood volume which facilitates oxygen and nutrient transportation.[29]

To those who say, "**but I drink water! There's water in my coffee, water in my beer, water in my Pepsi, water in my....**" Yes, but all those substances contain diuretics; diuretics make you urinate; frequent urination, because water is lost along with other liquids, can dehydrate you. Therefore, don't trust your mouth to warn you if you need water. Researchers counsel: drink six to eight glasses of water every day, more if you're physically active. (For the female officer forced to remove her gun belt for each trip to the lady's room, if this is too much liquid intake go with small containers of unsweetened fruit juice.) Drink it with every meal, order only water in restaurants and, in time, you'll realize it's the only substance that truly quenches your body's thirst. And drink it **before** you're thirsty!

VITAMINS AND MINERALS

Vitamins are organic substances required by the body that usually operate by activating enzymes. They are facilitators: functioning as catalysts for various chemical processes essential to good health. And even though their existence has been definitely known since 1947 (they were theorized many years before then), debate still continues concerning whether or not their ingestion via supplements is a health-enhancing necessity for the human body.

The fat-soluble vitamins A, D, E and K are stored within the body and are usually ingested along with fatty foods such as liver, eggs, milk and margarine and/or green leafy vegetables.

The remaining vitamins are water-soluble: the body excretes any surplus or unnecessary amount that has been ingested, so it's not possible to overdose on vitamin C, for example.

Nutritionists agree that a well-balanced diet will supply you with all the vitamins your body needs on a daily basis. However, if you smoke, added or supplementary vitamin C may be needed; similarly, heavy drinkers might benefit from additional B vitamins, specifically thiamine, niacin, pyridoxine and folic acid. Women using oral contraceptives may also need increased doses of B complex vitamins.[30]

Unlike vitamins which fulfill their function by promoting change, minerals actually become part of the body's structure. Bones and teeth are composed largely of calcium, while red blood cells are primarily made up of iron, for example.

Again, an adequate diet will normally supply all the mineral requirements needed, though mineral deficiencies are known most often among women: iron deficiencies occur in child-bearing-age females and nursing mothers who lose iron during the menstrual cycle resulting in anemia. And, as mentioned earlier, calcium deficiencies occur among women, a condition called osteoporosis which is further aggravated by a high protein diet.

GOOD FOOD—A NEW BEGINNING

Good nutrition begins by discarding old, bad and dangerous food habits. The benefits you derive will be noticed almost immediately but certainly within two weeks, **and** the benefits will be shared by your entire family.

For right now, understand a vital point: your bad habits took many years to develop; they are not going to vanish in a few days. So, again, go slowly and with moderation. Don't try to change every item of your weekly menu in a short time. Proceed gradually. If you've habitually skipped breakfast (or the first meal after you awaken), concentrate the first few weeks on restoring that extremely important component of your day back into your life-style. (I **know** you're "not hungry" then. That's because you've **conditioned** yourself not to be hungry. A week or two of eating that vital first meal and your appetite will return.)

Many people skip meals in the mistaken belief that the practice aids in weight maintenance or reduction. Actually the opposite is true. Besides lowering your blood sugar which causes irritability and nervousness, the additional hunger caused by meal skipping will usually result in your eating more than a normal intake when you do finally eat.

Remember, larger meals consumed before you retire are **more** fat-producing than the same number of calories spread throughout the day and preferably consumed long before bedtime. So skipping a meal consistently each day will help to make you fatter.[31]

Finally, some substitute foods and new practices to aid your transition; these consist of no or low cholesterol food choices that can be started now.

- No more whole eggs, or at best no more than one per week. If you crave fried eggs, eat the white which is protein and give the yolk to someone you don't like. There are commercially available alternatives that contain no cholesterol and are prepared as easily as scrambled eggs. Rather bland, so plan on building it into an omelet.
- **No** bacon, sausage or processed luncheon meats. No butter. Replace with polyunsaturated margarine which is usually sold in plastic tubs. Eat plain old-fashioned (not instant) oatmeal at least twice a week. It can lower your cholesterol.
- No shortening or cooking oil made with animal by-products. Replace with olive, safflower, sunflower or corn oil.
- Leave the salt in the shaker. In two weeks you won't miss it anymore.
- No whole milk. Two percent is good but still has too much fat. Skim milk is best. (I know what you're thinking. I couldn't stand the looks of it either, at first. But habit formation takes time. Skim gets colder than whole milk and believe me, blindfolded, you couldn't tell the difference between the two. The chalky taste you attribute to skim is in your mind, not your mouth.)
- No ice cream or no more than a moderate portion once a week. Substitute sherbet or light brands of ice cream which contain no cholesterol.
- Don't avoid red meats—moderate portions a few times a week won't hurt you, but get lean cuts and broil them.
- No more than two small coffees a day. When dining out you'll notice most good restaurants offer a wide variety of foods that can be fried or broiled. Just tell the waiter you want it broiled. Order water with dinner.
- Avoid foods awash in hollandaise or other creamy sauces.
- **Bring your lunch to work with you.** No more "handle one more call"

before you eat. No more fries with extra grease. You will **know** your food is healthy (and clean) because you brought it from home. Will you get kidded? Of course. **But,** show the kidders you're a leader, not one of the crowd.

And, for goodness sake, have a salad.

The benefits you'll derive from a sensible low fat/low cholesterol and high fiber diet include:[32]

- Less fatigue due to lower blood fats.
- Increased energy and endurance.
- Fewer headaches.
- No more constipation.
- No hunger pangs.
- Lower risk of degenerative diseases.
- Very possibly, a longer life.

So there you have it. If a little knowledge is the key that turns the lock, now you can open the door to your new, healthier nutrition habits.

For definitive good food information, I strongly recommend the book, **The Pritiken Promise.**

Chapter VII

DIETING TO GET FATTER

In some cultures obesity is regarded as the ultimate in beauty. The accumulation of body fat signals that you've arrived. It's recognized as an attainment of wealth, luxury and status. Sumo wrestlers, as an example, represent a pinnacle of athletic prowess to millions of Japanese. In point of fact, a sumo contest wouldn't really be sumo without the spectacle provided by those combatants and their mountains of quivering fat.

The study of body fat has not yet become an area of specialization within the medical profession. Because of this a physician's pronouncements concerning your flab tend toward the generic. **"You ought to get that stomach down,"** he or she will tell you. Or, **"Maybe it's time 'we' went on a diet,"** or something else innocuous like that.

In this chapter you'll see why it's so very difficult to permanently lose all the fat you've stored over a lifetime. An accurate understanding of fat as a component of your body is essential to the process of getting rid of it and replacing it with muscle tissue.

What follows explores diets (i.e. starving yourself to lose weight) and why they **never** accomplish a permanent fat reduction.

Human body fat is stored energy. You ingest more calories than you burn up in a day; those unburned calories are stored by the body as permanent fat.

Interestingly, it doesn't take a long time for this fat-accumulation process to take place. Eat a big dinner just before bedtime, down five or six beers before retiring, and in the morning you will be a fatter individual (if imperceptibly so) than when you went to bed.[1] Follow this routine year in, year out, and one day it dawns on you that you haven't seen your feet for a long time, that loafers are much easier to put on than tie shoes, and that your only view you have while prone at the beach is the blue sky and your belly.

A fat cop is a danger to himself and his colleagues, not to mention the public. There is absolutely **nothing** he can do as well as his trimmer brother and sister officers with the exception of sitting on an unruly prisoner to quiet him or taking a door off the hinges as a prelude to a raid.

Carrying unneeded pounds of fat greatly increases your risk of coronary heart disease. It greatly aggravates the condition of hypertension (high blood pressure); it contributes disproportionately to incidents of strokes and heart attacks and aggravates diabetes and respiratory ailments. Besides being ugly and useless and a terrible burden for the rest of your body to bear, it slows you down, if not in thought then certainly in action. That's a dangerous condition for a street cop to suffer. It can be fatal, not only to the heavyweight, but to his partners.

Fat cells in the body are stored in adipose tissue, pockets of fat located in the same places in men's, differing somewhat from women's bodies.[2] Most people always have the same number of fat cells; some people have more cells than others, still others have more fat **within** the cells.[3] Short of surgery you do not shed fat cells when you experience weight loss through dieting, for example. The cells remain; they merely decrease in size.

And, yes, fat tissue also nestles between your muscle tissues. That's the physical relationship of muscle and fat that produces the marbling effect in a cut of beef.

There are two critical considerations in understanding how much your body fat affects your fitness and health:

- **Percentage Body Fat** — Simply how much of your total body weight is composed of fat.
- **Fat to Muscle Ratio** — This is a critical relationship, particularly if you want to lose or maintain weight. Muscle tissue burns energy, fat tissue does so very inefficiently.[4]

The **percentage of body fat** can be measured in two ways. The most accurate is immersion in a tank of water, after first being weighed at waterside. Since fat floats, the percentage of you that's pure fat can be determined. A second, less accurate method involves the use of skinfold measurements using calipers on three areas of the body.

Obesity, in deference to the many height and weight charts in use around the country, is not a function merely of your weight or your height. Because muscle tissue is heavier than fat, it is possible for an extremely muscular individual to register as absurdly overweight through use of the charts, even though he or she is in superb physical condition.

Obesity is **solely** defined by the percentage of body fat:

- Males generally have between 10% and 19%. **Beyond 19%, you are obese.**
- Females have a higher body fat percentage than males: generally between 13% and 22%. **Beyond 22%, you are obese.** [5]

Let's consider a 180-pound male who has 12% body fat. That percentage equals almost twenty-two pounds of stored fat, which as you already know is dangerous, ugly and debilitating. Our guy has to carry these 22 pounds with him, everywhere, everyday, unnecessarily overburdening his heart, limbs, joints and lower back. And if you don't think 22 pounds is a big deal, get some small weights, 2½ and 1¼ pounds, put them in your pockets and walk around for a day: you'll get a graphic impression of the harm unnecessary weight inflicts. And, it should be emphasized, 12% body fat is **very lean by American standards.**

Where are the places on the human body where stored fat nestles? It's again different for men and women. But, the consistent and important factor is this: regardless of your sex, fat goes on your body in a pretty rigidly fixed progression. Body fat is stored **systematically** as the percentage of fat increases.

- In men fat goes first to the waist, then the arms, neck and face.
- In women the progression is more involved: first the inner then outer thighs, then the hips and buttocks; the stomach, the breasts, arms, neck and, again, finally the face.[6]

It's also important to know this: fat comes off your body in the **exact reverse** sequence in which it went on. So when you reduce your percentage of body fat through a weight reduction program, the first place it will become evident is in your face.

Additionally, knowing the progression of fat accumulation, it becomes easy to understand why it's often difficult for females to lose weight below the waist. It went on there first and it's the last place it's going to come off.

The fat-to-muscle relationship is also frequently misunderstood. If you're trying to lose weight or maintain consistent weight this ratio is critical: fat tissue cannot burn energy efficiently, ergo, muscular individuals can reduce any fat that accumulates quicker than an individual of average muscular composition.[7] Because females have a higher percentage of body fat to begin with (which equals a smaller relative amount of muscle tissue), an overweight female will usually experience much more difficulty losing fat than an obese male. This is, of course, a generalization but one that holds true in the great majority of cases.

It should also be noted: large thighs, for example, can be genetically inherited. Such a condition indicates the presence of more than the average number of fat cells. Reduction in the size of one's thighs in this instance might necessitate surgery.

Another frequently misunderstood process involves the weight lifter who ceases to exercise: do his muscles turn to fat?

It is impossible for muscle tissue to become fatty tissue. What does occur, with the cessation of hard muscle-maintaining exercise, the muscles atrophy (shrink) and in the presence of the same caloric intake, new stored fat **replaces** areas of shrunken muscle tissue.

The big stomach you may be hefting around hurts you in other, perhaps less obvious ways. The muscles of the lower back were designed to hold you more or less vertically while standing or walking; also to assist you, among other motions, in bending over and straightening up again. A heavy stomach bulging with stored fat pulls these muscles forward and down, directions of force that were not intended for lower back muscles.

Much lower back pain, then, could be more accurately diagnosed by a quick look at the individual's front.[8] The same physics applies in pregnant women as they pass their sixth month; more outward and downward pressure exerted equals lower back pain.

But police officers add a variable to the equation: the gun belt, weighing between five and six pounds (depending on whether you wear the Pancho Villa model with 3 speed loaders); this additional weight added to the large stomach area produces increased strain on the lower back muscles. Sliding in and out of the patrol car many times each day further aggravates this already deteriorating situation and it becomes small wonder that so many officers suffer from chronic lower back pain, or why back injury is a major cause of police disabilities and subsequent early retirements.[9]

Finally, besides being a real turnoff there is a definitive correlation that exists between the size of your waist and your longevity: that's why your chest and waist are measured during a physical prior to obtaining a life insurance policy. (Also, the **Surgeon General's Report on Nutrition and Health** noted correlations between obesity and higher rates of coronary heart disease, high blood pressure, diabetes and possibly some types of cancer.)[10]

Understand, these calculations are not mere flights of fantasy, they are actuarially computed in order to assist the insurance industry in continuing to amass piles of money. So the insurance people take these measurements very seriously and so should you. The statistical relationships are very clear: the larger the gut, the shorter the life.[11]

"But how much should I weigh?" you ask. Very simple. Assuming you were normal in weight when you stopped growing in height (not obese, not skeletal), **that's** what you should weigh today. So dig out your senior high school yearbook and take a good look at that youthful face. What you weighed then, you should weigh now.

"But I'm 189 now," you say. **"I was only 162 in high school. I could never go back to that. I'd be too puny and weak!"**

Really now, let's be a little analytical: how many of those pounds you gained represent valuable muscle? Unless you've diligently lifted weights or performed other exercises designed to increase muscle mass, none of it. If you're like most people **EVERY OUNCE YOU GAINED SINCE HIGH SCHOOL IS NOTHING BUT FAT!** And fat, as you already know, is nothing but trouble. It didn't make you stronger or a better cop. It just made more body with a trim person trapped inside.

However, don't run out to the gym and start doing sit-ups until you pass out. A final word about fat: you can't successfully attack it directly. You could, theoretically, do a thousand sit-ups a day and it wouldn't reduce the fat around your waist by even a millimeter, though it would tighten the muscles **underneath** the fat.[12] Remember, it went on your body systematically; it will come off (in reverse order) the same way, a progression of shedding it **without** dieting.

How much should you weigh? Here's a formula to help you determine your optimum weight.

Take your height in inches and

> **FOR MEN:** Times 4 Minus 128
> **FOR WOMEN:** Times 3.5 Minus 108

Men: If your dominant wrist is over seven inches around, you can add 10% to the total weight computed.

Women: If your dominant wrist is more than six and one-half inches around, add 10%.[13]

NOTE: Body builders **will** weigh more, since muscle tissue weighs more than fat.

Then, how much should you **eat** to maintain this optimum weight? Take the result of your calculation above and multiply it times 15 (13 if you're over 40). That figure is your average daily caloric intake.[14]

Now I know the body weight figure you just computed is probably going to upset you, but consider a **new you,** thirty or so pounds lighter than now, with a much reduced percentage of body fat and what that's going to look and feel like: to go from the Jabba the Hut of the **Gendarmerie** to the Fred Astaire of the **Federales.**

And anyway, even if you don't care about yourself, you should at least be considerate of your pallbearers.

The Dieting Hoax

Few societies in history have enjoyed such an abundance of food that obesity ever became a widespread problem. Ancient Rome comes to mind, at least among its aristocracy and other privileged classes. And, of course, Americans, many of whom, through ignorance, have elevated the act of accumulating body fat almost to an art form.

Ostensibly, this epidemic condition of obesity is a reflection of our national wealth. A recent government study showed that 34 million Americans are overweight.[15] Bad eating habits and a sedentary life-style also play a significant part. But to truly and simply characterize that which leads a normal man or woman from trim to tuba dimensions, only two factors have to be considered: how many calories do you **consume** vs. how many calories do you **burn** in a day?

Certainly, numerous other considerations play a part: heredity, life-style, metabolic rate, stress levels and so on. But I maintain, except in the severest cases, if you burn up as expended energy **all** the calories you consume each day you will stay trim, keep your percent of body fat within acceptable levels and never, absolutely **ever** be forced to undertake that senseless and harmful practice that's a perpetual cyclic life-style to millions of Americans: dieting.

Fad dieting is a subculture within our society. Literally tens of thousand of pages have been published lauding new and easier ways to shed extra pounds. Not surprisingly, many millions of dollars have been spent by those obsessed with becoming thin, staying thin or getting thinner. If you haven't noticed, diets are Big Business in America.

Now an outrageous generalization: Americans are a very impatient people and cops are often the most impatient of Americans. This translates to a chronic condition of the fidgets: what took you twenty years to accumulate you want to lose in three days. Or less. Hence, fad diets that advertise claims to unprecedented and quick weight loss seem an answer to your fondest hopes. Unfortunately, even if they perform as claimed, the fat, once shed, returns much faster than the last time. Yes, you lose the weight, but is the weight loss permanent? Mostly fat tissue? Healthy? It is none of these things. And, therein lies the essential fallacy inherent in the practice of starving yourself to lose weight. It simply does not result in a **permanent** weight loss of fat. And it is **not** a healthy thing to do. Starvation or quick-fix diets, when practiced by someone who is already chronically tired due to the effects of shift work, poor nutritional habits and prolonged stress, is an invitation to debilitation and disease.

Metabolism is the continuous process by which food is assimilated, energy is produced and oxygen is exchanged. Metabolic rates vary considerably from person to person; that's why some people can eat enormous meals and never gain an ounce while unfortunate others eat like birds and get fatter. A sedentary life-style largely contributes to a slow (fat-accumulating) metabolism.

Among humans the ratio of your fat-to-muscle composition is a critical one when weight reduction is considered. That's because muscle or lean tissue most efficiently burns energy taken in by the body. The more lean tissue, the more you can eat and the more efficiently food will be metabolized without fat accumulation.[16] That's why muscular males who do gain a few pounds at the waist can trim that excess off with little effort; normal males with a higher muscle-to-fat body composition ratio than females can reduce their weight easier than females and that's also why females who usually possess a higher percentage body fat than males experience the most difficulty losing unwanted pounds. Muscle tissue burns energy. Therefore, the more muscle you have, the easier it is to lose weight.[17]

Part of the difficulty in dieting to lose fat may very well be genetic in origin. Throughout the process of man's evolution, stored body fat had a purpose: it constituted the last reserves the human body could use to sustain life during prolonged periods of starvation conditions: famines, for example, or periods of economic or agricultural dislocation caused by warfare.

Stored body fat under those conditions translated to stored energy, just as it does today, something the body can transform, if necessary, to prolong life.

When you starve your body in order to lose weight a genetic trigger clicks and your brain perceives, and acts upon the premise, that famine is threatening your existence. Thus, in order to **protect** the stored fat tissue which is the absolute **last** reserve of sustenance, the brain causes the body to adapt. Within a week to ten days your metabolic rate slows. In the absence of sufficient nutrition the body burns glycogen, an immediately available energy source, at the same time as it sheds water in which glycogen is stored. Your initial weight loss, then, is mostly water.[18]

Once glycogen is depleted the body must consume its constituent tissue in order to compensate for the nutritional shortage you've imposed by limiting your caloric intake. But because of your built-in genetic safeguard, instead of only body fat being burned, muscle tissue is **also** burned for energy. And obese and sedentary persons will burn more muscle tissue than they burn fat.[19]

Think about it. Can you really afford to lose **pounds** of valuable lean muscle tissue, particularly since once you've attained or surpassed the age of 40 it is **extremely difficult** to replace? And this destructive and counterproductive process is repeated **every time** you subsequently starve yourself to lose weight!

There's still another set of reasons which interact to ensure that diets don't result in permanent weight loss. When you reduce your caloric intake from, say 2,400 to 1,600 calories a day, your body, in slowing its metabolism, initiates an adjustment to this reduction like an auto transmission shifting down to aid in climbing a steep hill.

By the third or fourth week of your diet the downshift adjustment is so complete that the body can now sustain life, if not perfect health, indefinitely on your new reduced 1,600 calorie-per-day intake.[20]

So after you achieve your weight reduction goal, feeling a sense of accomplishment for shedding those ugly ten or fifteen pounds, you quite naturally resume your old eating habits. But now 2,400 calories per day equals 800 calories too many; **the excess is immediately converted to new stored body fat!**

And, because you have shed valuable muscle tissue during your diet, the new accumulated flab makes your percentage of body fat increase. Thus, a year after the completion of your **successful** diet you are a fatter individual than before you attained your weight loss.

But that's not all: because you now possess less relative and less actual muscle tissue and because your dieting has further slowed an already sluggish metabolism, any further **future** attempts to lose weight will be progressively more difficult ones. Dieting has not only made you fatter but it has also seriously impaired your ability to shed weight in the future: a cause and effect that continues to make a bad situation worse.

This debilitating destruction of muscle tissue presupposes that sufficient muscle was available to be consumed in the first place. Yet in cases of extremely obese people, people who have dieted off and on over a period of years, such a supposition may not be valid.[21]

In the absence of sufficient muscular tissue, they are faced with yet another **famine** condition as the body searches for other tissue that can be converted to energy. It finds the heart, liver and other internal organs and begins to **consume** these. In extreme instances of prolonged starvation (the unfortunate inmates of concentration camps during World War II, for example), autopsies revealed internal organs of adults to be a fraction of their normal size: a man's heart the size of a walnut, for example.

Prolonged starvation diets practiced by those with low amounts of muscle tissue risk serious damage to their internal organs.

Similarly, those who **overdo** strenuous exercise without adequate caloric intake to compensate run the same risk. Doctor Kenneth Cooper discussed marathoners who, due to an inadequate caloric intake, had died, mostly in their sleep. This phenomenon, known as nutritional arrhythmia, resulted from starved heart muscles.[22]

Of course, if you are willing to maintain your caloric intake at minimal dietary levels (1,000 calories a day), your dieting will result in permanent weight loss. But those minimal levels must be maintained **for the rest of your life!**[23] You must keep in mind, however, the more prolonged the diet, the more severe will be manifest the symptoms of fatigue and exhaustion, a general lack of vigor that can lead to chronic depression, a wonderful condition for an already sleep-deprived, highly stressed and usually otherwise unhealthy cop to endure.[24]

And chronic exhaustion leads to an even more sedentary life-style, further reducing your opportunity to burn off calories in a healthy and permanent way.

Contrast this sad scenario to one where your lean muscle tissue increases, as does your metabolic rate, so that you can eat and drink as you want without gaining an ounce, because there are healthy ways to permanently lose that fat and feel like a teenager again through a process called aerobic fitness. It will create a new, alert and vigorous you in concert with sensible eating, adequate rest, stress-coping techniques and moderate exercise, all interacting.

It's called aerobic exercise and if it sounds like a miracle, it is.

Chapter VIII

ALCOHOL

Sometimes it's possible to know a subject too well, or to think you do. Alcohol is a good example. Police officers deal with the fallout from the drug just about every day. Like any other people, cops form opinions over time based on observation and experience. And, to round out their knowledge on the subject, just like most other folks, most cops drink. Therefore, there is nothing new on the subject you might think. The subject is closed.

Or maybe not. Police experience with drinking and the drunk bestrides a wide range of human behavior: mopping up the carnage of an alcoholic-fueled frenzy; drunk and disorderly arrests; suicide attempts and successful suicides; victim passed out with a lit cigarette and burned the house down; or alone in the cell block, decked in vomit, crying; the one with tremens, screaming wide-eyed, like the devil squatted in his cubicle.

All this, then eight vodkas and a fistful of barbs running insane; and more: a sixteen-year-old knocked 110 feet from point of impact, both legs broken, skull crushed on the concrete. Hit and run. Drunk driver.

Then come your personal experiences with the stuff. Relaxation, coming down, euphoria, instant goodness in your bloodstream, a stimulant for all senses and seasons; mind like a razor's edge; humor (**"you must be drunk, I see two of you"**); vanquisher of inadequacies, of shyness, from taciturnity to brilliance in just three beers.

All this is alcohol and more. So when you think you really, **really** know the subject, maybe a lot of important information's gotten by you. And if it has, that's not surprising.

Experts in the field still bitterly debate the causes and the cures of alcoholism. Like a police officer, confronted with the problem in the flesh, the suspect, ranting and not a little dangerous, while perhaps the cop himself is nursing a high, tight hangover; suffice it that there's often too much emotion intervening to objectively evaluate cause and effect.

Alcohol abuse is one of those unfortunate facts of life that's so pervasive most folks don't pay it too much attention, unless, of course, it touches, in one of numerous ways, your life or the life of a loved one.

There are ten million alcoholics in the United States, yet most function as well-accepted members of our society. Indeed, the typical American alcoholic is in his or her mid-thirties, resides in a good home, has a good job and a family.[1]

Alcoholism is also a growing phenomenon among teenagers, three million of whom are estimated to have drinking problems.[2] It costs American industry billions of dollars a year in lost time, accidents and impaired productivity, and it costs the medical insurance industry billions more. Yet it is a widely misunderstood malady and the subject of continuing debate precisely as to its causes: Heredity? Environment? Or a varying combination of both?

Part of the misunderstanding necessarily stems from the fact that 70% of all adults drink, most without developing an addiction.[3] Unlike regular heroin users, for example, 100% of whom will become addicted, only about 10% of alcohol users become alcoholics.[4] This is an enigma that has long puzzled researchers and has led many alcohol treatment professionals to perhaps less than comprehensive conclusions.

What is not debated is this: alcohol is a drug called ethanol that, upon ingestion, travels immediately to the stomach. There, about 20 percent continues on through the stomach wall directly into the bloodstream. The remainder is transferred more slowly, from the stomach to the small intestine, then into the bloodstream.[5]

One ounce of 100-proof whiskey can be processed by the average human body in a single hour. Though this varies considerably due to body size and sex, the amount of food present, the concentration of the drink, and so on. Once in the bloodstream, the drug will be distributed into every organ within minutes. In small amounts as it enters the brain, alcohol has immediate behavioral effects. The drinker is stimulated, elated, euphoric and energetic. At this level of ingestion, alcohol is a pleasant stimulant that actually **improves the drinker's performance and thought processes.**

Larger succeeding amounts (and the amounts differ widely among individuals) begin to disrupt the brain's electrical and chemical circuits; more complex, often unpredictable behavioral changes ensue as the drug begins to disrupt the function of the central nervous system. At this point intoxication, with resultant lack of motor coordination and judgment, begins.[6]

From the first drink the body works to remove alcohol from its system. The primary site of alcohol elimination is the liver. Upon entering that organ the alcohol molecule is attacked by an enzyme which quickly converts it into acetaldehyde.[7] This highly toxic compound, if allowed to accumulate, will produce a rapid pulse, nausea, dizziness and mental confusion. The second stage in the liver's alcohol-elimination process employs another enzyme which transforms the poisonous acetaldehyde to acetate which is then converted to carbon dioxide and water, both easily eliminated by the body. This progression of chemical reactions occurs in nine out of ten drinkers.[8]

It is precisely at this point where the proponents of heredity as the sole predeterminant of alcoholism begin their argument, for studies done among various ethnic groups have concluded that an inverse relationship exists among two important variables: the number of generations alcohol has been used by a group and the ability of its population to metabolize acetaldehyde, the toxic substance.

Among native Italians, for example, in a culture where alcohol has been present for over 7,000 years, the incidence of alcoholism is extremely low. Conversely, in native Americans, Indian and Eskimo subcultures where alcohol was introduced only about 300 years ago, the rate of adult alcoholism is extremely high, sometimes surpassing 80 percent.[9]

The heredity factor is given additional credence by studies done of offspring of alcoholic parents: one group raised in the home of the biological (alcoholic) father/mother and the others raised by unrelated families. The incidences of subsequent alcoholism were the same for both groups.[10]

Medical testing has confirmed the inability of some individuals to metabolize acetaldehyde as efficiently or quickly as the general population. Since acetaldehyde is very toxic and very volatile, anyone who cannot metabolize it could not drink alcohol, right? Wrong.

Because of the human body's marvelous ability to adapt and through a complex interrelated series of metabolic changes, cells in the alcoholic's body actually change their structure in order to accommodate alcohol. This restructuring results in cells which eventually **prefer** alcohol to any other nutrient; cells actually **addicted** to the drug.[11] This adaptation is physiological in origin and creates within the alcoholic a high tolerance for the drug.

Thus, alcoholics experience a dramatic increase in their tolerance in the first stages of alcoholism. This increased tolerance allows an alcoholic to drink large amounts without suffering mental impairments that would generally follow in persons whose bodies normally metabolized acetaldehyde. The alcoholic's high tolerance level exacts a heavy price, however. Over time the earlier adaptation of the cells leads to their destruction. Yet, the addictive physiology now operating requires the alcoholic not only to continue his drinking but oftentimes to increase it. An increase in tolerance, then, can be a first warning sign of alcoholism.[12]

The adaptation of the alcoholic's cells follows a pattern. As time and the addiction progresses, an alcoholic's body needs to ingest more and more of the drug in response to the needs of his adapted cell structures. Ultimately, he must drink merely to feel, act and function like a normal person. Abnormal drinking patterns have become his every day behavior. The obsession with a next drink is due not to psychological flaws but in **response to a physiological imperative.**[13]

In the late stages of the disease the alcoholic's liver ceases to function. It is too congested with fat to detoxify his blood, and poisoned blood flows throughout his body profoundly and adversely affecting his physical health, behavior, even emotions.

Ironically, the fatty diseased liver of a chronic alcoholic or a heavy drinker results, in part, because alcohol is the only drug that can also accurately be described as a food. In fact, in terms of the number of calories it supplies, alcohol is a particularly rich food source. One ounce of pure alcohol imparts about 170 calories, equivalent (in calories only) to a broiled lamb chop, a glass of milk or a sweet roll.[14]

These calories are quickly available for conversion to the body's energy needs. Unlike fats, protein and carbohydrates which require hours of chemical reactive restructuring before they can be utilized as energy, alcohol's quick release into the bloodstream provides the body with energy almost immediately.[15]

So whenever alcohol is present within the body together with food, the liver has a choice of which to convert to energy. Because the chemical process to convert alcohol is so much simpler, the liver **always** opts to use the drug and convert the food also present into stored energy or fat.[16] This occurs not only within alcoholics but in anyone who drinks a significant amount.

As the fat accumulates it crowds the liver cells, many of which suffocate and die. With time the liver itself begins to swell, becoming, over time, inflamed, a condition called alcoholic hepatitis. Continuation of drinking at this point will inevitably result in cirrhosis, a liver so clogged that is can no longer fulfill its many life-sustaining functions.

High levels of triglycerides from the partially metabolized food also circulate in the bloodstream, hastening the buildup of fatty deposits within the arteries.

And, even though alcohol can be burned by the body as fuel, the drug itself lacks amino acids, vitamins and minerals. Without these nutrients, all of the body's cells lack the ability to replace damaged parts, create new cell materials or continue functioning as healthy cells.[17] The nutrients from normal food have been ignored by the body when stored as fat, or their assimilation into the cells has been blocked by alcohol's devastation of the cell structure, so the body cells are malnourished and incapable of normal function.

Thus, it is that even if a heavy drinker eats balanced and nutritional meals he is still a chronically malnourished individual who needs vitamin and mineral supplements to maintain his health.

If bad health is more often an individual's choice, it is also the result of various interacting factors: insufficient sleep, inadequate nutrition, sedentary life-style and so on. The work and life-style of many police officers tends to encourage poor life-style choices, which cumulatively result in the degeneration of the individual's physical health. Cops who endure all the other physical and mental stresses of their profession and who attempt to cope by frequent use of alcohol, voluntarily drop their potential for good health down another significant notch or two.

Though few studies deal specifically with the alcoholic cop, it is safe to assume, based on these studies, that over one in five officers suffers from a serious drinking problem. If true, that equates to 100,000 alcoholic police officers in the United States![18]

This is not to say that all heavy drinkers are addicted to the drug. On the contrary besides alcoholics, authorities in the field recognize a difference between regular drinkers:

- **Problem Drinkers** who are not alcoholics (that is, their body processes acetaldehyde in a "normal" manner) but whose use of alcohol creates psychological and social problems for themselves and/or others.
- **Heavy Drinkers** who drink frequently and in large amounts; **may** be an alcoholic, a problem drinker or a normal drinker with a high tolerance for alcohol.[19]

The abuse of alcohol is an insidious process. It can literally sneak up on you after many years of even moderate alcohol use. Danger signs include: gulping drinks; the inability to stop once you've started; regular times for drinking; self-neglect and neglect of family or job responsibilities; persistent physical ailments and frequent memory loss or blackouts. These last do not involve a loss of consciousness but rather a total inability to remember what you did or said during a period of alcohol ingestion.

If you've ever called a friend from the night before to find out how you acted because you have absolutely no recollection, that's a blackout. You can spot victims of blackout fairly easily. They're the ones wandering the neighborhood the next day, looking for where they parked their cars the night before.

There's still a stigma attached to women alcoholics and heavy drinkers that's not present for men. Whatever else drinking is or is not, it is still widely regarded as part of the masculine domain where the observation, **"he drinks like a fish"** does not impart a totally negative connotation. Some even perceive it to mean, **"what a man!"** Not so if it involves the female of the species.

Heavy drinking and intoxication are pretty universally frowned upon as unfeminine behavior at best and at worst she's a you-know-what. Currently there are about two million women in this country who would classify as alcoholics and the rate of female alcoholism is actually increasing at a much faster rate than that of males.[20]

Women with drinking problems face additional gender-based disadvantages over and above the threat of social condemnation. The degenerative physical effects of heavy and sustained alcohol abuse manifest themselves much sooner than in males.

And there's a curious and unexplained statistical insight that, perhaps, reflects society's double standard: nine out of ten men leave alcoholic wives; nine out of ten women **stay** with alcoholic husbands.[21]

There are other obvious differences, as well. Women usually point to a particular life crisis or trauma as a single primary cause triggering heavy or alcoholic drinking: prolonged family stress; loss of a loved one; sexual problems or a medical crisis are most frequently cited as causes. Women find it more difficult to seek and remain in treatment than do men.[22]

Female police officers are often faced with more pressure to drink with their colleagues than would ordinarily be the case in most other occupations. Precisely because of this pre-applied pressure to indulge as an essential of off-duty socializing, even a social drinker can frequently surpass his or her alcohol limit.

Just as frequently, some primary or secondary result of drinking lands an officer in trouble with his superiors either through relatively small infractions like lateness or calling in sick, to being arrested for driving under the influence, and just about every other transgression in between. **Knowing** alcohol exempts none of us from its dangerous and harmful potential.

These occurrences usually diverge from the norm, however. Habitual heavy drinking assesses its penalties every day in ways that, like stress, interact to weaken and undermine health. Weight gain is probably the most noticeable, though even that usually progresses so slowly it is difficult to pinpoint an exact time when you got your large belly: one day you simply realize that you're heavier than you've **ever** been before. If you've been a heavy drinker for years, a four-or-more-times-a-week drinker, it probably wasn't the alcohol calories that grew that stomach but rather the food that could not be metabolized for energy in the presence of alcohol, and was converted to fat and stored around your middle.

How that diminishes you as a person and a cop you already know, or perhaps not. Men who are heavy drinkers experience a diminution in the size of their testicles, decreased production of the male hormone, testosterone, and, in extreme, but by no means unknown cases they develop breasts![23] So much for the macho aspects of heavy and prolonged drinking. Think about these symptoms, because the odds are excellent you know at least one middle-aged male who is experiencing them.

Drinking to relax and unwind is an accepted practice throughout our society. But the sleep that follows heavy consumption, though it may seem profound, actually falls far short of imparting adequate rest. This is because the deepest sleep phase, REM's, is simply not attainable when a large amount of alcohol is present in your system at bedtime.[24]

So though you find yourself dropping off almost immediately, you awaken more tired than before you went to bed. Then, off to Roll Call. . . .

There's no doubt that alcohol is a powerful drug capable of inflicting enormous harm if abused. Vigilance and moderation in its use are necessities that minimize risk for all persons except alcoholics, who simply **must** abstain from alcohol.

Coping through alcohol use rather than through healthy life-style decisions will soon result in a new cause of stress and illness, manifest in physical, social and sometimes psychological ailments as well. Depend on it: whatever problem you bring to alcohol, alcohol **will** make that problem worse.

Chapter IX

ALIENATION

The informal police group comprises a subculture not unlike a crew sailing a ship at sea. Networked to various degrees with your colleagues, both at work and at play, you provide each other with a kind of security blanket woven from commonly-held beliefs, perceptions and experiences. It is an insular arrangement that protects, but assesses a measure of alienation from the larger society.

Is the act of withdrawal from family, friends and society a conscious one? If so, when does it begin? Is it a predictable process? Or does it lap like waves on a beach, perpetually advancing and retreating?

Most probably like the incredible complexity of human behavior, alienation evolves on an individual basis, alternately fed or famished by the instant's dominant compelling influence.

However it progresses within the police officer, withdrawal towards the far shore of alienation has touched many of us. It is as if we chose to say, **"no one can really understand what I've endured."** No one but the endurer, of course, and his defense is to deny the feelings turning him ever inward and away from the world. Because in truth "they" can never hope to know the fear and pain that you've successfully masked from them all the years of your adulthood.

It is significant that long before most men or women have decided on a lifelong career, most police officers have already been on the job six or more years. The average age for entrance on duty is only twenty-two and most young officers are already married and beginning a family.[1]

Unfortunately, armed though they are with awesome authority and fulfilling responsibilities that would daunt an older adult, these young people are often not themselves fully matured as human beings or as spouses or even as an ego. Many surely have not yet attained the self-awareness, self-confidence or self-acceptance that precedes personality formation.

In the absence of emotional preparedness they absolutely need strong and nurturing guidance; a network of support, indeed protection, that can ward off the emotional, administrative and physical dangers and can steer the young officer to a plateau of departmentally and socially acceptable values, ones that are realistic **and** attainable.

Yet in most cases the very people who can provide this help tend to further isolate the young officer from the mainstream of society. Why? Because the young officer instinctively seeks support only from those who can fully comprehend what he or she is experiencing: older officers who are products of the cauldron themselves and who, as likely as not, have long been immersed in the murk of cynicism. The older cops welcome the child-adult newcomer with the resigned misgivings that accompany their role as veterans and teachers.

So, as the youth progressively experiences the terrors and heartaches, the adrenalin-induced highs and moribund depressions, the scornful looks and contemptuous comments of the society he has sworn to protect (with his life, if need be), there is there for him or her an older hand who has experienced it all before; experienced it and learned from it and who now dispenses the wisdom that proceeds from that experience. This is a powerful role, more than mere friend or parent or even spouse; the elder's word is often **law.**

The younger is soon shaped by these experienced cops, thoroughly redeveloped as a self and as a persona with totally new outlooks, perceptions and opinions. Within a very few years the youth's pre-police identity, which took 20 years or more to form, has all but disappeared, replaced by a composite value system inculcated by his elders.

This indoctrination results in a powerful, insular and nearly all-encompassing **brotherhood** which, representing authority within our society, paradoxically resists and often resents authority when it is directed towards them.

"Forget everything you learned in the Academy" is their lesson number one.

Lesson two: the street can be a marvelous bitch, always the same, always varied; peopled by a cast of players, some so fascinating they seem unreal; almost like fictional characters.

The street is sometimes exotic, always entrancing, and occasionally seductive. It is also complex; an unforgiving environment, multi-textured:

it demands a lot of learning, a lot of studious analyses just to find out who the players are. And time is always short.

Police work can, if you let it, absolutely consume every waking moment of every day, for not an hour passes that something doesn't change: something new happens or there's another development to be absorbed. Indeed, before too long the day's images are returning in your sleep: action sequences and repressed fears coming at you night after night; graphic violence, a continuous recurring theme. Violence met first with inadequacy; and, of course, violence ultimately answered with even more violence: your own.

To say the experience can be all-consuming is to understate the obvious, particularly for a young officer wanting to do well; caught up in a flood tide of fervor and exalted expectations. Nothing, absolutely nothing in his young life could have prepared him for this.

And for a time other interests in life may pale by comparison. Old friends don't seem as interesting; mom and dad can't comprehend the changes they are seeing; even the spouse and children begin to seem a little too mundane, as time spent with them begins to diminish. The only true reality is the street and other cops and bad guys: cuffs, occasional fisticuffs; patrol; interviews; delinquent reports; roll calls, turn-ups, lock-ups, try-ups and maybe a few beers with the guys when we get off.

"What day is it, anyhow?"

Over the months and years the job comes home silently. **"I don't want to worry her (or him)"** becomes the universally recognized rationale for shutting out the spouse. First from your **fears**, later from your frustrations. The job swallows the majority of your waking hours and most of your energy.

Within the first five years the pattern of behavior is set: **"Don't talk to me when I first get home"** you tell her; **"let me come down."**

The children, used to being scolded for being like children while daddy's asleep, now learn to tiptoe through the living room. But kids are very adaptable creatures and in scarcely no time they instinctively know when, and when not, to approach you.

Mom's adaptable too. Though if anybody bothered to ask her, this police work crap is starting to wear thin. Though she (probably) rarely complains but rather settles into a routine that has her raising the kids:

driving them; disciplining them; reassuring them; and for most of every day, doing it virtually alone.

So the children of cops are often raised through and past the age of adolescence, having more in common with kids raised in single-parent homes. If mom works too, so much the worse. And if she's also a cop, God (or grandparents) help them all.

Holidays take on a new, slightly negative cast: which ones **won't** we have as a family this year? Easter? Not **Christmas** again! And extended family get-togethers, Christenings, weddings and the like, well you knew all that when you signed on, didn't you?

In fact, meaningful time away, spent just with your family can become as excruciatingly anticipated as your first real sexual encounter. And, as you count down day after endless day towards the morning of your family getaway, you pray that you won't get a court summons for smack in the middle of your week's vacation, or that the seven-year-old bomb you drive keeps its transmission together, or that one of the kids doesn't get sick again, or that **you** don't.

What you perhaps fail to notice is this: because of the nature of your work, such a simple necessity as a vacation has taken on unbearable significance, becoming time for you to fulfill all the promises made to spouse and to children. A year or more's emotional IOU's all coming due during a single week in July. More claims for affection and attention than you can hope to honor.

The few previous family vacations have been paragons of heightened, and unrealistic, expectations, sandpapered nerve endings (**"What was that grinding sound? Did you get the fluid put in?"**) and epic frustrations: (**"Wow! This is Chopper 13. In 12 years of reportin' traffic conditions we have never seen so many cars backed up for so many miles!"**)

And you, with blood sluicing through your temples, who just a week ago could think of nothing but some blessed time away from the uniform and the patrol car, now can think of nothing so much as being back at work where at least you can pop the blue light on and avoid a traffic back up altogether!

Even if you don't love your work (and most undeniably do not love it), returning to it after an absence holds all the bittersweet charms of a high school reunion. At the very least here you have an adequate and pretty accurate handle on that human quality all humans occasionally need to quantify: **who you can trust.**

Cops are hardly exceptions to this human need. In point of fact, I sometimes think this need was first invented solely by them.

Okay. First, if the world doesn't assort itself into tidy piles, well than you have to do it for yourself, don't you? After all, there are too many imponderables out there; too many, many things that, if approached the wrong way, for instance, can very definitely get you hurt.

So, **first** thing, most of the cops are okay. You might not want to invite some of them home, but there've been a few times when you were happy to see one of them coming to save your ass. That's got it then: cops are definitely okay.

Now for the rest of the world. Let's see: some of the store owners on my beat like police. That's a plus. And they're helpful if you need a place to sit and have a quiet coffee. Okay, the merchants are all right guys.

Mentally scanning the remaining populous of the rest of your domain you begin to realize that of the numerous contacts you've had with civilians, not a whole lot of them have been of the uplifting sort, the kind of personal contact that leaves you with a warm glow afterwards. Many were victims which, at best, makes them stupid; others were too demanding (unreasonably so) of your time and attention; some were downright arrogant: pointing their fingers at you, raising their voices. Then there were those who were outrightly hostile, to the point of confrontation.

Now, you were raised to believe that there's some good in everyone and that maxim still holds validity. However, your contacts with people have tended you toward a rather different set of conclusions:

>**"Yeah, I guess most people are okay, but God, sometimes they can sure act like asses."**

Over the years this belief crystalizes with some of its temporizing edges sanded down until one day you realize that, essentially, most people are asses. They're dumb or, worse, crooked; arrogant or dangerous. Sometimes they're **all** of those things.

So there you have it. What the Police Academy could not impart to you concerning the vast complexities of human nature, you have taught yourself, with a little influence from your colleagues, to be sure. How's that again? Right: cops are okay, most civilians are not.

Freed now from the vagaries of muddle-headed humanitarianism, you can go forth to do police work, unencumbered by any unorthodox thinking that can get you hurt or worse. Your newly hatched **Theory of**

People in the Universe has distilled all possibilities of life into two alternate life forms, greatly simplifying what could have been an otherwise nasty business of constant analysis and probing thought.

The wonder is most officers I've known temporize this extreme and do deal with Mr. Citizen humanely, politely, even occasionally going out of their way to aid, protect and assist him. This is not to say that the people have not been preclassified, only that most cops have more humanity and sensitivity than they themselves would readily admit to having.

At any rate, an **us** and **them** mentality exists and it is reinforced by the work schedule. People assigned to rotating shifts or merely shift work, according to research results, are much more prone towards group insulation. This includes a bonding with other (same shift) group members; the presence of in-group humor and resentment at the attempts of others to become more involved with the group.[2]

Among cops there exists a group-held perception known as territoriality. This, in turn, breaks down to become each individual's parcel of turf: his or her beat, a geographic slice of jurisdiction jealously guarded by the officer even to the exclusion of fellow officers where **handling** one's own beat is a primary responsibility. The practice, when proficiently done, underscores an element essential to male bonding.

Qualities revered in such a group include all the human attributes usually ascribed to hunter/warrior societies throughout history. Physical courage is foremost among these, as are honesty (within bounds), leadership, trustworthiness and keeping faith with the group and its members: looking out for each other regardless of physical dangers or departmental prohibitions (and not just while on duty).

The trappings of such a male-dominated subculture can exert horrific stresses on female officers. Stated tersely, it's harder for a girl cop to gain acceptance from her peers. Some never do. In that one way, the police profession, unfortunately, mirrors the larger society. Women are usually not treated fairly; women are subjected to pressures most men simply cannot understand; women must perform better than an average male counterpart in order to be regarded merely as adequate. Though a competent diligent female officer performing consistently well will, in time, probably be accepted, it is acceptance hard-won and it is granted and viewed as an **exception** to the norm.[3]

Regardless of the status she achieves, however, if the female officer displays solidarity with the group and trustworthiness, she is accorded membership **privileges**. In many instances, her acceptance is, if not provisional, then tenuous. She is more quickly subject to group condemnation or censure should her performance not conform in things professional. Even the best female officers often evolve into walkers-on-eggshells, too quick to divert conversations apparently heading up the wrong ladder. The good police girl knows when to keep her mouth shut and is expected to do so much more often than are her male colleagues.[4]

Male-dominated clannishness thrives, if not flourishes, fulfilling a function precisely because most of its members perceive a need for that function. It is a symbiosis of persons, banded together for mutual protection. The extent to which it fulfills the needs of all its members across racial, ethnic and sexual lines is usually in direct correlation to the effectiveness of its informal leadership.

To the formal organization of which it is an integral part it can be a force for vast potential good or dangerous organizational divisiveness. So too is the range of its effect on its members, each of whom must submerge a portion of his or her identity as the cost of membership in good standing.

Too often the professional and social demands of the informal organization relegate the officer's family to a secondary status. This is understandable: there simply are not enough hours in a week to fulfill all one's job-related and family responsibilities. When shift work enters the equation you find yourself on a carousel, which allows you to see your family members in a predictable sequence but only in passing. Quality time spent with your spouse and children becomes increasingly rare. That spent with non-police friends becomes mostly a memory.

It is, I think, a truism that a healthy, vital and interactive family life is the absolute cornerstone to the physical and mental health of any individual. Having around you people you love and who in turn love and support you is what life is all about.

Love is nurtured and kept healthy through a continuous process of communication, between spouses and between children and their parents.

Unfortunately, the archetypical male police officer is, by definition, non-communicative; a stoic throwback to an earlier era when ignoring one's pain was counted as a positive male virtue. This trait, taken together with an officer's genuine desire to insulate and protect his family from the frightening aspects of his work, works instead to corrode the marriage from within; So does the difficulty of coping with shift work.

Research suggests these problems are transferred to wives and children.[5] The marriage falters as mutual expectations begin to erode, as the non-police spouse starts to perceive that continuing his or her existence, replete with few or no mutually shared experiences and with divergent life goals, is a self-defeating exercise that must cease.

Or, the long-suffering police spouse must decide relatively early on in the marriage if the reality is worth the deprivation both for herself and for the children. If she is a self-sacrificer who holds to some prospect for a brighter tomorrow, she will stay. Her life distills itself to a train station mentality: **"Things'll get better when we get to the next stop."**

Where the officer has the informal support group to count on, the spouse is left unsupported, very often handling the problems attendant to any marriage with little assistance other than a paycheck.[6]

Add frequent alcohol usage to this scenario and the results become predictably worse.

For the informal group often expects its members to drink together. Shift change parties are the highlight of the group's social calendar, and even though they can produce much aberrant behavior, they are less destructive than the practice of drinking at shift's end **"to come down"**; much more destructive to the cop and his family because it takes place much more frequently than the shift change get-together. And, because of shift work, it takes place at what the 9-to-5 segment of society would regard as odd hours: eight thirty in the morning, for example.

Without even seeming to at first, these get-togethers gnaw away further at time you might have spent with your family. Many of the breakfast drinkers are divorced; others separated, some from their second spouses. Often they have no one to go home to.

After hours spent away, you arrive home too exhausted to do much of anything but fall into a shallow unsatisfying sleep, prepatory to arising around 9:00 p.m., and beginning the cycle anew, only a little more exhausted and a little less wanting to hear of things relating to your family.

The adaptable kids see all. They see much more than you think they see: abnormal home life has become their normalcy. With some twists. The cop father can be a draconian disciplinarian motivated as he is to absolutely protect his family from all the evils in the world. He does not ask, he **interrogates** his children, assuming their guilt often before a word has been spoken. **"I know what you've been up to"** is implied. This live-in but absentee parent is good for money and grief and little else, a condition that ultimately creates a vast reservoir of resentment and further non-communication between parent and child.[7]

It only takes a few years and the unlined face of the neophyte cop has puffed and aged a decade or more; around his once trim waist an envelope of fat is growing. The greatest change is not visible, however, for it lies behind his eyes, his opinions and conclusions of the world and all therein. He has become a perpetual searcher, judging everyone he meets from the parish priest to the kid who mows his lawn in terms of **"what is he after?"** Unceasingly, often sardonically, he searches for the hook, losing, in the process, his ability to say, **"I'm sorry. I was wrong,"** or **"I love you,"** because the final stage of the alienation process occurs within the individual: a form of self-hatred and self-destructiveness that's difficult for anyone else to breach, much less heal.

In his book, **The New Centurions,** Joseph Wambaugh depicted the ultimate result of alienation in the characterization of Andy Kilvinski, former cop's cop, now retired. Sitting alone in his furnished room he contemplates his best friend, a .38, in the knowledge that everything in his life: family, friends, are now gone. So he eats his best friend. And therein, with more drama than reality, nevertheless, is underscored an important point. Membership in the informal police group cannot continue past retirement. It is ended then and all the time invested, all the laughs, all the beers, all the scrapes and all the stories told, equal nothing.

Chapter X

BODY RENEWAL

For many the words **to exercise** mean something dirty; it dredges up painful memories: boot camp calisthenics, August wind-sprints; police academy push-ups and worse. Despite the fact that this country is experiencing a fitness revolution, about four out of five police officers do not exercise at all.[1] Part of this, no doubt, is due to a real or a perceived shortfall of time.

And part of it, too, is due to a basic and simple inertia, an, **"I've been like this for fifteen years and I feel okay"** mentality (best to pat your belly when saying this).

Besides imparting a negative connotation, the term exercise is a widely misunderstood concept. Some folks believe that mowing the lawn or washing the car or even aggressive grocery shopping will provide all the physical exertion necessary for a minimal level of health and fitness.

Others take the stairs instead of the elevator whenever they can, setting their hearts on **race** by the third or fourth floor and earning, in the process, a florid complexion and very little else.

Regardless of the source of your phobia concerning exercise, one critical point must be made and understood: if you perceive it as distasteful and as drudgery, you're defeating yourself before you begin. Indeed you probably won't begin. And your body, designed for strenuous physical activity and engineered to enable you to walk across continents, will continue to deteriorate, aging you prematurely and cutting short your vitality and, very possibly, your life.

Again, knowledge is the key, knowing the simple facts of cardiovascular fitness. Above all, you've got to understand that fitness and trimness are not going to be yours in a few days. What took many months to degenerate can be repaired but only gradually, the result of practiced moderation and steady effort.

Exercise should not be a pain but rather a source of joy and self-pride, providing benefits out of all proportion to the time invested. So, shed your impatient American outlook and commit to a new, healthy, lifelong life-style.

And, if you cannot instantly drop your dread or distaste of the subject which is certainly understandable, at least read this with an open mind and keep in mind there must be a very good reason you see thousands of joggers, walkers and cyclists out there. Is it minutely possible that these millions of exercise fanatics might know something you don't? Are they experiencing something so elemental, so invigorating and so positively addictive and uplifting that they'd rather skip a meal than miss a workout?

What **do** all these people know that you don't?

About fifteen or so years ago researchers began noticing that a negative correlation existed between incidence of heart disease/heart attack and regular strenuous aerobic exercise. Since then other research has confirmed: regular aerobic workouts significantly lower your risk for heart attack and provide other substantial health benefits.[2]

One study conducted of 17,000 Harvard graduates as they've progressed through life since graduation recorded similar findings with an unexpected twist: those who've regularly exercised since leaving school have experienced (as a group) a dramatically lower incidence of mortality even when their respective life-style choices or family history would seem to predispose them to an above average risk of premature deaths.[3]

The presence of high density lipoprotein or HDL is the primary contributing factor in this life-sustaining and life-threatening phenomenon. Researchers discovered inordinately high levels of this so-called **good** cholesterol in the blood of marathon runners and other endurance activity athletes years ago. High HDL levels in your bloodstream provide you with more assurance of a longer healthier life and afford significant protection against both heart disease and atherosclerosis.

HDL accomplishes these by performing three vital functions:[4]

- It scours the interior artery walls, removing soft fatty deposits.
- It then coats the artery walls preventing future fatty buildups.
- Finally, it flows through your bloodstream, removing fats from your blood.

Pretty impressive? HDL is a kind of miracle substance because nothing else known to man or medicine can so effectively clean your arterial network. Of course, it's always been around, but only relatively recently have its beneficial effects been fully understood. A raised level of high density lipoprotein is the essence of good insurance and good sense. If it were for sale, pharmacies the world over would be besieged by people tossing baskets filled with money to buy the stuff.

But it's not for sale. It's manufactured by your body. And there's only two ways you can guarantee you have sufficiently high levels of it to promote a long and healthy life. The first way is by limiting your intake of high cholesterol and saturated fat foods.

The second and most reliable way is through regular aerobic exercise.

Aerobic exercise is sustained physical exercise; taking in oxygen and raising your heart rate. An optimum level of your exercising heart rate is achieved when you:

> Establish your maximum heart rate through the use of this simple formula: 220 minus your age equals your maximum heart rate. So then, the maximum heart rate for a 40-year-old is 180. Multiply 180 by .7 (for 70%), which equals 126. This figure is the exercising heart rate or E.H.R. and it represents the number of pulse beats per minute the exerciser must attain, in the presence of oxygen, to ensure aerobic exercise is taking place.[5]
>
> Some writers on the subject advocate attaining 80% of the maximum heart rate. If, however, you've been sedentary for a long time prior to beginning an exercise program, moderation and common sense should prevail. That equates to attaining only 70% and maintaining it at that level even after your physical conditioning improves.
>
> To monitor the E.H.R. during your workout, take your pulse at the carotid artery (that's in your neck) with your first two fingers; count the pulse beats while watching the second hand of your watch (or use a stopwatch). Count the number of beats that occur within ten seconds then multiply by six. For example:

Pulse beats in ten seconds =   21
Multiply by   6
                                 ————
Exercising heart rate = 126 beats/minute

This level must be maintained **for a minimum of twenty continuous minutes** in order to achieve a minimal aerobic benefit. Twenty minutes is your target exercise duration for the first month or so. With practice over a several-week period you won't have to monitor your pulse so frequently; experience will tell you when the rate is being achieved.

It's also important to note you must be able to talk in a normal conversational tone throughout your aerobic activity.[6] This is not to say that you won't experience some shortness of breath. That, of course, is natural. However, if your breathing rate ascends to the point of panting as in **breathing is the only thing in the world you can even conceive of doing at that moment in time,** you have departed from the realm of aerobic exercise and find yourself performing anaerobic exercise.

This activity is harmful; it causes an oxygen depletion, then an oxygen debt and it achieves the direct opposite of what you are striving to achieve. Anaerobic exercise occurs when the fat, badly out of shape police officer rushes up four flights of steps then wrestles with a bad guy. It's the **blue lips** look, you've probably seen (or experienced) it. The anaerobic state of exercise is typically attained by an individual who, for fifteen years or so nestled before his T.V. in a lounge chair, then woke up one morning determined to run 7-minute miles around the track. After the second lap he could tell you his name only with great difficulty so enormous is his need for air. He has thus accomplished two significant negatives: piling up an oxygen deficit and further strengthening his cherished belief that exercise in general is an exquisite form of torture in which he will never again take part.

Just as important as deciding to perform aerobically is the choice of activity. Obviously, it's got to be something you like to do or you're not going to stick with it. Running or jogging are the obvious choices but they're certainly not the only ones and as high-impact workouts, not the best. Others include aerobic dancing, bicycling, jumping rope, swimming, and walking, to name the obvious ones.

And, you'll notice the list does not include bowling, baseball, softball, touch football, tennis (unless you and your opponent are both quite adept) and weight lifting (though there are exceptions to this). These activities do not fulfill the requisites of aerobic exercise, because they do not elevate your heart rate to the E.H.R. and keep it there for a **minimum of twenty minutes.**

Three primary considerations govern the quality of an aerobic workout:

1. **Frequency** — How many **times** per week.
2. **Intensity** — How **hard** you exercise.
3. **Duration** — How **long** you exercise.

Generally speaking, the equivalent of walking twelve miles a week will provide you with a very good level of the aerobic benefits attainable through physical exercise: cardiovascular health and raised HDL levels among others.

Beyond the **fifteen**-mile-per-week point, there is evidence that some of these benefits actually decrease.[7] So, a good level of aerobic fitness will be attained by walking/running or their equivalent three miles per day, four times per week.[8]

A point that cannot be overly stressed is this: warm-ups and warm-downs are of critical importance in the exercise process. They are needed to minimize the stress experienced not only by your heart but by your muscles and joints as well; and their importance increases with increasing age: like warming your car engine on a frigid morning.

Warm-ups and warm-downs are actively accomplished through light stretching and easy calisthenics to particularly affect those areas of the body about to bear the brunt of the chosen exercise. The presence of sweat during and following warm-up is a good indicator that the desired effect has been achieved.[9]

Avoid rapid jerking motions. Perform the warm-up/down with fluidity and ease of motion. Keep in mind, the purpose is to raise your heart rate, gradually and easily, to the E.H.R. and maintain it through the workout. The less conditioned heart demands gradual, not violent, changes in activity level.

Warm-downs following the workout also can do much to prevent torn and tender muscles and damaged aching joints. Remember that your body's flexibility **decreases** with age.

The definitive work on aerobic fitness is Doctor Kenneth H. Cooper's book, **The Aerobics Program for Total Well-Being,** one I recommend. Working in his sports fitness center in Dallas, Texas, Dr. Cooper and his associates have conducted definitive research concerning cardiovascular fitness adding much to our current knowledge of the topic. The relative figures regarding the frequency, intensity and duration of the following activity descriptions were taken from **The Aerobics Program** and are included in order to facilitate your employing more than one method of exercise at comparable levels of each.

Walking: a personal and **recommended** favorite. Safe for all ages and most physical conditions, it's always **available** and does not require expensive outlays for equipment. Walking is gaining in popularity precisely because of these reasons and the fact that injuries are rare occurrences.

Some authorities maintain you burn more calories per mile walking than you do running or jogging, since these faster activities trigger a metabolic overdrive that burns calories at a slower rate.[10] Walking is smooth, fluid and a natural activity unaccompanied by the crush and shock of pounding on asphalt or concrete. Also you will take in more oxygen per mile than running or jogging simply because it takes longer to cover a mile. Excellent aerobic and cardiovascular conditioning can be gradually achieved within the first ten weeks by progressing to four times per week, three miles per day. Time elapsed per mile should be between fourteen and fifteen minutes per mile.

Running/Jogging: the difference between these two is time elapsed to cover one mile. If accomplished in nine minutes per mile or less you are a runner; more and you are a jogger. The aerobic benefits are comparable to walking but are attained quicker (more of Type A behavior).

Running can cause serious injuries if improperly done, and plenty of people nationwide have suffered as a direct result of this form of exercise. Despite the risks, it attracts a multitude of adherents and has done much to increase the nation's health consciousness and the fitness level of millions.

Be certain to buy or use well-made shoes, manufactured specifically for running; anything less does not sufficiently cushion the shock of feet pounding on a hard surface. Bargain running shoes are not a bargain.

Swimming: probably the best all-around aerobic and muscular exercise. The problem is you obviously need something to swim in and you need to know how to swim. Much less potential for injury (unless, of course, you happen to drown), and, assuming you have access to an indoor pool, it's an activity that can be pursued year-round, regardless of weather conditions. It does not burn stored body fat, however, as do other aerobic activities, an as yet unexplained phenomenon.[11] Swimming nine hundred yards in under twenty-three minutes four times per week is comparable in aerobic conditioning to walking twelve miles per week.

Bicycling: another personal favorite, it's an activity more like fun than exercise, capable of easily elevating your heart rate to the E.H.R. Also adds an element of excitement and danger, particularly when done in big-city traffic.

Obviously, a good ten-speed bike is not cheap and, except in the most temperate of America's climates, you're probably going to be limited to six or seven months of the year, decreased (for safety's sake) by rain or snow days. To achieve E.H.R. you've got to travel about fifteen miles per hour. Biking is increasingly becoming more popular with fitness enthusiasts. Though it minimizes the pounding, serious injuries, falls or other accidents can, of course, cause serious injury and deaths are not unknown. A good level of aerobic fitness can be achieved after you've attained the ability to pedal seven miles in around twenty-eight minutes, four times per week.

The Court Sports: handball, basketball, racketball, et al. provide an element not present in most other activities: competition, which probably will make the time go by faster. Again, these require a minimal level of proficiency and even at that there's more stopping and starting which inhibits maintaining a consistent E.H.R. Contact with other players, walls and playing surface are all good possibilities as is the potential for contact injuries.

Also, if you're over thirty-five years of age court sports can frequently provide you with unfamiliar sounds emanating from your joints, particularly the ankles and knees; these sounds are caused by the often violent stop/start motion necessitated and inflicted on a human body that is beginning to lose some of its youthful suppleness. Want a preview? Wrap a handkerchief around a pencil, then snap it in half. That's what a torn tendon sounds like. One hour about four times per week is equivalent to walking twelve miles.

Weight Lifting/Body Building: aerobically speaking, these two activities are quite different. Preparing for competitive weight lifting through use of heavy weights is anaerobic in nature. However, multiple sets containing numerous repetitions (12–20) and minimal weight with minimal rest between sets (60 seconds) will provide decided aerobic benefits, elevating your heart rate to the required E.H.R. and keeping it there consistently throughout the workout.

There's a catch, however: you need to be in excellent physical condition to begin with in order to safely perform aerobic weight training.

If weights are your thing, however, don't be discouraged; they can provide you with valuable assistance in achieving both cardiovascular health and muscular development. Simply engage in one of the forms of aerobic exercise already described for approximately three months; once you've attained a good level of cardiovascular fitness, begin your weight routine to add muscle tissue. The more muscle you can amass, the lower your percentage of body fat and the more effective your body becomes in the process of energy conversion. Thirty minutes three times a week will result in aerobic fitness in conjunction with another aerobic activity.

Skipping Rope: if you think this is for sissies you've obviously never tried it. One of the most effective ways of quickly elevating your heart rate. It takes some coordination, but it's cheap and can be done indoors.

The aerobic value varies with the speed you apply. Ninety to one hundred ten steps per minute for about 17 minutes equals a three-mile walk.

Achieving an E.H.R. lasting about forty minutes four times per week will get you in very good cardiovascular shape. These times are exclusive of warm-up and warm-downs. So, realistically, plan to budget four hours per week on your chosen activity. That equates to about 2% of the 168 hours in a week or one hour in fifty. That's a minimal commitment for the benefits you'll derive.[12]

Strengthening the Heart Muscle: regular aerobic exercise causes the heart and the vascular system to increase in size and efficiency. As a result each pumping stroke of the heart muscle forces a greater volume of blood through the arteries. The well-conditioned heart is stronger and needs to beat fewer times per minute to force the same volume of blood. This benefit is manifest by the low resting pulse experienced by those who regularly exercise. A pulse rate in the high fifties, low sixties range is quite normal and **an indicator of excellent cardiovascular health.** As a comparison, consider that the average person's pulse beats 72 times per minute; that of a well-conditioned person beats 60 times. In a single week that equals 120,960 additional beats which the poorly conditioned individual's heart must beat to perform the **same function** as the well-conditioned heart. In unmedical terms this is called wearing out your pump prematurely.

Lowering Blood Pressure —Since the number, size and elasticity of the vascular system are improved, a stronger heart pumping blood through wider, cleaner arteries needs to exert less pressure per stroke. Decreases your risk of stroke.

Increasing Your Energy and Endurance: since a more efficient and higher volume of blood delivery ensures a greater supply of oxygen within your body; simultaneously it stimulates new and healthy tissue growth.

Better Quality Sleep and a Calmer You: partially due to the pleasant tiredness that comes from sustained vigorous activity and interacting with a lower resting pulse—the adequately rested body is a calmer and more able-to-cope mechanism. Adequate sleep is a prerequisite to good health. Kiss chronic fatigue good-bye.

Permanent and Painless Weight Loss and Weight Control: metabolism can be defined as the conversion of food into energy and the rate at which that energy is expended. It varies greatly among individuals as to age, sex, and physical condition among others. Regular aerobic exercise enhances that tissue's ability to burn stored energy. The body expends calories even when you are at total rest, say, an average rate of 60 calories per hour. After you've walked three miles in prescribed time you will (again depending on your age, condition, etc.) burn about 350–400 calories. But following the workout the rate of calorie expenditure does not immediately return to 60 per hour but returns gradually over a two- to four-hour period.[13]

In essence, your body continues to burn calories at an **accelerated** rate for up to four hours following the exercise. This process is accentuated as your conditioning improves and your muscle tissue is altered and increased. So endurance athletes who possess low body fat and high conditioned muscle mass can actually burn calories at an accelerated rate even when they're sleeping![14]

Additionally, the chemical recomposition which takes place in well-conditioned muscle tissue pays another valuable dividend.

Under ordinary circumstances, your body's energy needs are supplied by glycogen or stored sugar. Well-conditioned muscles experience a proliferation of mitochondria which increases the muscles' ability to burn fat as fuel.[15] This beneficial effect takes place past the three-mile calorie burn level and only in well-conditioned muscles. You have got to get in shape and stick with your program past the third to the sixth month for this to occur.

Thus, fat metabolization is the antithesis of the "quick fix" approach to reducing weight through diet or exercise. Since many people abandon their programs within a few months, they never experience this remarkable benefit.

After your muscles have become well conditioned, walking the fourth and subsequent fifth mile will trigger this response. The energy being burned, glycogen, will be replaced by the conversion and expenditure of stored body fat.[16] It is at this point that you'll begin to see the fat literally melting from your body. Officers who have followed this method of weight reduction were astounded by three unexpected advantages over traditional dieting: (1) the weight loss was painless; (2) it did not adversely effect their mass of muscle tissue; and (3) they could eat normal meals without the risk of additional fat accumulation. Aerobic exercise and **sensible** foods resulted in a permanent weight loss unaccompanied by fatigue, weakness, nausea and other unpleasant characteristics of diets. As their percentage of body fat declined, the remaining muscle mass grew as a proportion of total body weight, allowing for an accelerated rate of fat reduction and bolstering future ability to quickly lose any new accumulation. Adherence to an aerobic program for a lifetime, however, will guarantee there will be no future fat accumulation and ensure your weight loss is a healthy and permanent one! Other benefits include:[17]

Increased Blood Volume which supplies more hemoglobin, thus increasing the blood's ability to transport more oxygen.

Lessened Risk of Osteoporosis, the weakening and deterioration of the body's bone structure, which particularly afflicts post-menopausal women. Weight-bearing aerobic exercises include running, walking, weight lifting, skipping rope and aerobic dancing, as these activities strengthen and thicken the bones.

Significant Protection from Heart Disease since H.D.L. levels increase which lessen the risk of developing atherosclerosis.

Stress Reduction due to your lower heart rate response to stressful situations. Also, exercise, particularly at the conclusion of a stressful day, works by **flushing your system** of the hormonal secretions which have accumulated, restoring your chemical balance and reinvigorating you. This method of stress reduction, unlike the use of alcohol or other drugs, enhances rather than diminishes your levels of energy. Aerobic exercise also acts as a powerful tranquilizer enabling you to much more successfully cope with life's emotional bumps and bruises.

Increased Resistance to Infectious Diseases through better overall health and reduced stress levels.

Better/Safer Job Performance. Being a fat and/or out-of-shape cop is like playing Russian roulette with an automatic. It endangers the officer and his or her partners. It isn't a question of **if** you'll get hurt, merely of **when.** Alertness, agility, strength, stamina and mental acuity are all benefits derived from good physical conditioning.

Treatment of Depression: the phenomenon known as **runner's high** is described as an exercise-induced euphoria and feeling of extreme well-being sometimes visited upon vigorous frequent exercisers. In recent years the source of these feelings have been traced to the secretion of powerful hormones called endorphins which are released from the pituitary gland. Endorphins are morphine-like substances available inside the body to aid in controlling pain. Instances of profound depression have been linked to low endorphin levels, so for years psychiatrists have been treating this illness by prescribing forms of aerobic exercise.[18]

There are, of course, other benefits to be derived: pride in your new appearance; the indescribable joy of feeling good, having lifted the veil of chronic fatigue from your eyes; and a new feeling of self-confidence.

But all these benefits have to be experienced to be believed, not just read from a printed page. There's a brighter, better world, waiting to be discovered by your newly sharpened senses and perspectives. All you have to do is experience it. Then you, like millions of other Americans, will know the reasons behind raising some sweat. And know, too, the joys of a positive and healthful addiction.

First, remember: **common sense** and **moderation** must govern your decisions, and you must recognize that what you've chosen to begin is a significant start on a new life-style. As such it's got to be a realistic assessment of the activities you are willing to perform for the rest of your life.

Similarly, set goals for yourself that are realistic and attainable and be mentally flexible enough to be able to alter or amend those goals as your physical condition improves. Chart your progress with the eye of a realist and the heart of an optimist and practice the art of gradualism. Take it one day at a time.

It will also be beneficial to plan alternative aerobic activities during periods of extreme weather. On windy days when the temperature is below 20 degrees it might be advisable to perform an indoor exercise. Above 20 degrees or so remember to layer your loose-fitting clothing, since several layers provide additional warmth due to the warmer air trapped between each layer.

Remember also that more than half of your body heat exits by way of the head: it's your body's chimney, so a warm, snug hat is essential when you brave winter elements. Protect your skin on windy, raw days by applying a thin smooth coat of petroleum jelly or similar protective coating. And make certain you've thoroughly warmed up before beginning.

When summer's in full heat, particularly if you live in an area that produces frequent high humidity coupled with high temperatures, not to mention trapped vehicle exhausts, head for a swimming pool rather than try to run or walk. But if you feel you must exercise outdoors in such unhealthful conditions drink a pint or more of cold water before you begin, start slowly, and go in the early morning or after the sun's gone down.

Clothing should be cotton or mostly cotton, loose fitting and very lightweight; with bright colors or white worn in hours of darkness. And again, if your feet are going to be pounding on pavement, invest in good quality footwear and soft absorbent cotton socks no matter what time of the year. Quality running shoes (I use them for aerobic walking) are worth the price, another fact you have to experience to fully comprehend.

You will undoubtedly find, despite all your precautions—thorough warming up and down, listening to your body, not overdoing—that some muscle soreness will accompany your early efforts. And yes, this represents progress. You have stressed and moved parts of your body in unfamiliar ways. By taking special note of the body areas particularly affected by soreness you can, through trial and error, reveal inadequacies within your warm-up and warm-down and stresses peculiar to your selected activity.

Muscle soreness immediately following a workout is usually due to an accumulation of lactic acid in the tissue.[19] This is a result of anaerobic exercise and indicative that you either did too much or did it too fast or both.

Soreness which occurs twelve to forty hours following the end of your workout is probably due to muscle ischemia: microscopic tears caused by overstressing the muscle tissue in the absence of sufficient blood supply.[20] Though both types will probably occur, it's important to recognize they are temporary; as your conditioning improves, the causes of muscle soreness will disappear. And an adequate warm-down as intense as your initial warm-up will lessen negative effects. It also must be emphasized: the older you are, the more steady and comprehensive must be your warm-up and warm-down.

Prolonged accumulation of fluid in your joints should be attended to by a physician. Such an occurrence will probably dictate an alternative exercise routine.

Progressive physical development through exercise is achieved by overloading much the same way that muscle tissues are enlarged by stressing the target muscle to the point of muscle failure. Progressive exercise will produce a larger and stronger muscle.

If your goal is to achieve a minimal level of cardiovascular fitness, for example, then a **gradual program** tailored to that goal that is realistic and attainable will fulfill your wants within a ten-week period. Overloading, in essence, does not mean working your body to a state of exhaustion within the short term. Rather, set intermediate goals to accomplish a little more today than you did the last time you exercised. In this manner you'll accomplish overload without endangering your health. Remember, down time due to injuries is discouraging regardless of your age or degree of fitness.

Once your desired level of fitness is achieved, you need only maintain the program at the desired level, walking twelve miles per week performed in four 3-mile alternate daily workouts, or an equivalent.

A word about traversing hills: much of the difficulty is psychological in nature, seeing how far ahead is the summit that brings relief. Staring down minimizes this grief by lessening your mind's ability to perceive you're on an upgrade; the ground before you will actually appear to be level. It's crazy but it works.

If you hate the idea of walking hills (which means you're a fine, intelligent human being like me) to increase resistance, wear a fanny pack with anything weighing about a few pounds carried inside. The slight additional weight added to the resistance exerted by gravity will enable you to attain your E.H.R. **after** you've attained fitness.

Several final and important considerations: aerobic exercise lowers your blood fats and increases the H.D.L. in your blood. However, these effects are obviously not permanent ones; they occur and remain only for **twenty-four to thirty-six hours following your last workout**.[21] For this reason some writers on the subject strongly recommend exercising four times per week (every **other** day) in order to ensure the continuity of these positive benefits. However, it is possible to attain **minimum** cardiovascular fitness by exercising, exclusive of warm-ups/downs for twenty minutes, four times per week.

The question of **"When do I do it"** is a fair one. Remember, you are only going to devote about four hours a week to your exercise. So budget the time **you** most want to use. It obviously doesn't have to be the same time each day (indeed if you're on rotating shifts it **can't** be).

But only **you** can determine what is best. If a spur of the moment decision works for you, then that's the best time for you to do it. Knowing that a workout **every other day** means three workouts the first week (Monday-Wednesday-Friday) and four workouts the second (Sunday-Tuesday-Thursday-Saturday). Go with what feels good to you. Finally, keep in mind that proponents of the **no pain, no gain** philosophy have nothing pertinent to say to you on the subject. Moderation and going slowly will ensure your goals are met and maintained without injury. Pain simply should not play a part in the process.[22] Let your physical exertions be a personal celebration of life, not a detested activity you can't wait to finish.

SOME FINAL THOUGHTS

If you're over forty your life has spanned the time from when physicians were held in near-reverential awe by most people until now, when they are frequently (and often unfairly) excoriated. Being a cop you've probably already reasoned that the truth lies somewhere between these two extreme views.

Hopefully after digesting the information in this book, you've decided that the wisest course is to keep yourself well so that you don't **need** to see a physician. That goal is an attainable one.

However, **before** you embark on an ambitious program of self-improvement through exercise and modified sleeping and eating habits, do everyone who loves you a favor:

Go to a physician you trust, a doctor who takes the time to explain things; one who answers questions to your satisfaction and whose office accepts your group medical insurance, and get a thorough, unstinting show-all, tell-all physical examination! Also,

Tell him or her all about yourself and your profession;

Include the fact that you're going to begin rather strenuous physical exercise;

And **then** if he or she says it's okay, begin your life-style changes.

Like so many other items in life these aforementioned seem **so** reasonable and sensible, but most people simply will not take the time **or** spend the money to do them.

It's important when embarking on a bold new life-style; one that will result in a dramatically made-over-for-the-better-new-you that, in the process, you don't drop dead from the unaccustomed exertion. Dropping unexpectedly dead will absolutely rob you of the benefits you would otherwise derive from exercise.

Make **no** mistake: waddling onto an asphalt track, wearing brand new running shoes, carrying a body encased in ten (or twenty) years' accumulation of blubber and starting to run makes as much sense as backing into a holdup at a liquor store.

Sedentary people who attempt strenuous exercise without gradually attuning their bodies first **do die every year.** Don't be one of them.

And, if you have reached or attained the age of thirty-five, make up your mind to get a thorough physical examination **every year** for the rest of your life. Think of it as an oil and lube.

A prominent portion of your physical will consist of a comprehensive blood examination. In the absence of some familiarity with the significance of terms and their relationships to each other, the resultant blood analysis will probably result in your doctor saying, "**Ed, your cholesterol is 235. That's a little high. See what you can do to bring it down to normal.**"

"**Uh, what's normal?**", you'll probably ask.

"**220,**" the doctor will say. "**Yes, 220 is average. Of course, 210 is better. But 220 is normal.**"

For **Americans**, the doctor should (but probably won't) add, "**Remember, though, America is the home of the double bacon and cheeseburger.**" That fact alone has got to tell you something. American doctors are **conditioned** by high cholesterol values.

So what is good? Get and keep your cholesterol below 200 and you will dramatically lower your risk of heart disease, particularly if you're a male![23]

At the same time a **high** cholesterol count, in the absence of any other information, might **not** be dangerous.

Remember, a relationship exists between total cholesterol and **good** cholesterol, high density lipoproteins or HDL. Remember also HDL is the only substance capable of cleaning off your artery walls and protectively coating them against future fatty buildups. Relatively higher HDL levels among pre-menopausal females is believed a primary reason that females experience far fewer heart attacks than men.[24]

High HDL levels can be **genetically inherited** as well, and there exists a definitive correlation between high HDL levels and long-lived individuals around the world.[25]

The relationship of cholesterol with HDL is a very simple one. Take these two figures from your blood analysis and divide total cholesterol by HDL. For example, my most recent blood tests showed cholesterol at 177 and HDL at 50. Therefore, 177 divided by 50 equals 3.5. This is a very good ratio, demonstrating the beneficial results of exercise. Generally speaking, the **lower** the ratio, the **better** your health.[26]

Chapter XI

HOLISTIC LIFE-STYLE

Nobody can know where they're going if they don't know the starting point. You may think you're already perfectly attuned to those things in your daily environment that make you crazy. Chances are, for a variety of reasons, you are not, perhaps because the stress is caused by a loved one or by a situation that should not bother a **real** man.

An accurate self-assessment of your environment, **all** things: food, sleep, exercise, relaxation and others that affect you and your physical and mental health, takes a bit of knowledge and a ton of honesty.

Modern medicine, the marvel of technology that it is, cannot be the total answer to your quest for health and fitness. The reasons are twofold. Because doctors are taught to treat **sick** people, rarely do they practice, rarer still do they espouse preventive medicine. **Well** patients usually do not interest a doctor.[1]

Also, specialized medicine and its disregard of the **total** man or woman, including working environment, nutritional habits, sleep patterns and more, often **treats symptoms, not causes.** Yet, we know that we are products of an incredibly complex interplay of environmental, physical and emotional factors. To ignore these will usually result in an incomplete, often inaccurate diagnosis.

Your doctor, for example, should be totally conversant with the subject of nutrition and how foods affect physical well-being, even emotional health. Most do not know these effects because most physicians apparently receive only rudimentary instruction on the subject of nutrition.[2]

True holistic fitness requires **knowing** your physical, mental and spiritual self and keeping all three in synch **and** in harmony with your environment. It's a tall order, but once attained, it ensures that you keep yourself well so that you don't have to see a physician (other than for your annual physical). Remember: it's really no mystery why two-thirds of all cops' visits to their doctors result from ailments that are **psychosomatic in origin.**

These ailments manifest themselves usually after prolonged periods of unrelieved stress and usually in your body's most vulnerable component: severe headaches, for example, or ulcers. Like the weakest section of a submarine's hull that implodes under unrelenting pressure, ignoring the pain from your vulnerable point, be it head or chest or intestines, can ultimately destroy **all** of you.

And yet, even as children, many of us were conditioned to ignore pain, to function despite discomfort. This is a societally imposed stricture (much less prevalent with children nowadays, you've probably noticed) that ensures most people show up for work most days. It is not a bad thing until carried to absurd and often dangerous lengths. And it is compounded by the cop's inculturation: the **John Wayne** syndrome, a phenomenon which affects many police officers, often to their physical and emotional detriment, and which severely and dangerously circumscribes behavior deemed **acceptable**, allowing small hurts to go ignored or ill-treated until they become larger, more dangerous ones.[3]

Regardless of origin, self-destructive behavior patterns must be identified and be re-directed into healthy behavior. To do less or to do nothing, abrogates your nature as a primarily intellectual being, besides curtailing one of your most precious rights: freedom of choice.

The very first step involves a depth of self-awareness rarely achieved by people.

To begin, keep a diary that specifies daily activities and your physical and/or emotional reaction to each. To make it all inclusive, head each page with:

1. Day _____   2. Shift _____

Reactions

3. **Time**   4. **Activity**   5. **Place**   6. **Consumed**   7. Phys./8. Emot.

Numbers one through three are self-explanatory.

Number four, **Activity**, will include **anything that acts upon you:** an argument with your spouse, for example, a fifth cup of coffee, a car stop, **or** anything that you are **acting upon,** arresting someone or conversing with someone.

The purpose of a long-term diary, besides the obvious one of recording your activities, is to create highly personal data that can be analyzed in the long term; **not** to identify stressors that you know, but to isolate and recognize **those of which you are scarcely aware.**

Number six will require you to list all food/drink consumed every day not only to heighten your awareness of bad eating/drinking habits but also as an insight to how food and drink can further intensify both good and bad physical and emotional reactions to other, seemingly unrelated, things.

Number seven, **Physical Reactions,** should include solid biofeedback data: a racing pulse, for example, dilated pupils, sweaty palms, muscle tension (this list requires true diligence and self-awareness. You'll probably be surprised at the frequency of occurrence, particularly if you're a Type A personality to begin with).

Number eight, **Emotional Reactions,** should describe those feelings the rest of the world never sees of you. These represent that part of you hidden behind those expressionless eyes, the aloof police officer, playing the role of Mr. Emotional Detachment, the way you've trained yourself to react.

If this daily effort strikes you as tedious, it is. If you further think it silly or useless, it definitely is not. Maintain and update the diary (in a **very** safe place, of course) and, over a period of months, you will look back and see things that will amaze you about yourself: recurring patterns of destructive behavior that need to be changed. Through this process of self-awareness you'll find your starting point, a mental self-image that will lend you some motivation to begin the process of healthy life-style change.

Implicit in the process of self-awareness is the need for self-love, a recognition of you as a unique creation and a valuable and contributing member of the society of mankind. Recognition, too, of the fact that you have probably never scratched the surface of your potential for intellectual, physical and spiritual growth. And that the time to begin applying that vast unused potential is now.

Implicit in the process are a few fundamentals of **daily** behavior, habits ingrained and practiced among long-lived peoples the world over who have remained vital and active all their days. Research has identified seven life-style characteristics practiced by them.[4]

All:

1. Ate breakfast every day.
2. Ate three meals every day and avoided snacking.
3. Enjoyed 7 to 8 hours sleep every night.
4. Kept their weight to a minimum.
5. Drank in moderation or not at all.
6. Did not smoke.
7. Exercised at least three times a week.

The Stress Management Program offered by the F.B.I. National Academy enumerated various ways to reduce the effects of stress, each of which, interestingly enough, also contributes to redefining your environment and your place within that environment. These methods foster a creative and positive degree of selfishness: yes, a caring for **you** in order that you can become a better spouse, parent, cop and friend.

First, however, you must remember and practice a simple truth: **you are not responsible for your environment.** You are **only** responsible for your **reaction** to your environment.

Accepting and living this simple truth will go far towards your healthy adaptation to your surroundings, be they pleasant or otherwise. Then:

- Plan some idleness every day.
- Listen to others without interruption.
- Read books that demand concentration.
- Learn to savor food.
- Have a place for your personal retreat at home.
- Avoid irritating, overly competitive people.
- Plan leisurely, less structured vacations (and mini-vacations).
- Concentrate on enriching yourself.
- Live by the calendar, not the stopwatch.
- Concentrate on one task at a time.[5]

In effect, take charge of your surroundings to the reasonable extent that you can. Don't let the controllable aspects of your life run your life for you.

Self-knowledge, then, and a little self-discipline are the lock and the key to achieving true holistic life-style; a new and healthy way of living in harmony with your environment at the same time that you nurture the physical, mental and spiritual you.

So there it is.

Though the principles are not simple they **can** be grasped with a minimum of effort: grasped, embraced **and** incorporated into a new and healthy life-style.

Because you **are** worth the effort.

NOTES

INTRODUCTION

1. *Law Enforcement Officers Killed and Assaulted*, Federal Bureau of Investigation, U.S. Department of Justice, 1988, pp. 3, 43.

Chapter I
COPS: MYTHS AND HUMANS

1. Katherine W. Ellison, Ph.D. and John L. Genz, M.P.A., *Stress and the Police Officer*, (Springfield: Charles C Thomas, Publ., 1983), pp. 28, 29. Also, James C. Coleman, "Life Stress and Maladaptive Behavior," *Stress and Police Personnel*, Territo & Vetter, Eds. (Boston: Allyn & Bacon, Inc., 1981), p. 29.
2. Ellison & Genz, pp. 17, 18 and p. 16, "Much research shows that role expectations play an important part in determining behavior in all aspects of life."

Chapter II
SLEEP DEPRIVATION

1. Martin C. Moore-Ede, Frank M. Sulzman and Charles Fuller, *The Clocks That Time Us* (Cambridge: Harvard University Press, 1982), p. 335.
2. Joseph LaDou, "Health Effects of Shift Work," *The Western Journal of Medicine*, 1982, p. 527.
3. LaDou, p. 527.
4. LaDou, p. 527.
5. Robin Dodge, "Circadian Rhythms and Fatigue: A Discrimination of Their Effects on Performance," *Aviation, Space and Environmental Medicine*, 1982, p. 1131.
6. Moore-Ede et al., p. 335.
7. Moore-Ede et al., pp. 330–334 and "Shift Work and Health, A Symposium: *U.S. Department of Health, Education and Welfare*, 1976, p. 201. Robert D. Caplan cites "...disruption of life patterns of shift-like environments can affect serum cholesterol and serum glucose, both risk factors in coronary heart disease."
8. Lawrence E. Scheling et al., "Chronobiology and How It Might Apply to the Problems of Shift Work," *Department of Health, Education and Welfare*, 1976, p. 119.
9. Wilse B. Webb and C. Michael Levy, "Age, Sleep Deprivation, and Performance," *Psychophysiology*, 1982, p. 275.
10. LaDou, p. 525.

117

11. Jadwiga Wojtcak-Joaszowa, M.D., *Physiological and Psychological Aspects of Night and Shift Work* (Cincinnati: *U.S. Department of Health, Education and Welfare,* 1977), p. 26.

12. M. Brand et al., "Clinical Study of Retired Shift Workers," *U.S. Department of Health, Education and Welfare,* 1975, pp. 404–405.

13. Robert D. Caplan, "Social-Psychological Dynamics in Shift Work: Discussion I," *U.S. Department of Health, Education and Welfare,* 1976, pp. 206–208.

14. Paul E. Mott, "Social and Psychological Adjustment to Shift Work," *U.S. Department of Health, Education and Welfare,* 1976, pp. 145, 147.

15. LaDou, p. 526.

16. Mott, pp. 145–149.

17. Wojtaczak-Joaszowa, p. 28.

18. M. M. Ayoub, "Shift Work and Health—An Ergonomic Approach," *U.S. Department of Health, Education and Welfare,* 1976, p. 187.

19. C. Nilsson, "Social Consequences of the Scheduling of Working Hours," *U.S. Department of Health, Education and Welfare,* 1976, p. 494.

20. William H. Kroes, Ph.D., *Society's Victims — The Police* (Springfield: Charles C. Thomas, Publ., 1985), pp. 130–133. "In considering the 1950 data (Guralnick, 1963), another relevant and appalling finding is evident: there were almost twice as many deaths (94) by suicide as by homicide (54). [A statistic that continues to this day]... "Further, it is known that the figures on suicide for policemen are artificially low.... "The data on mortality presented above was from the year 1950. What of today? All the evidence indicates that the [suicide] problem for police is worse than ever...."

Chapter III
STRESS

1. John G. Stratton, *Police Passages* (Manhattan Beach: Glennon Publ. Co., 1984), pp. 106–109.

2. Katherine W. Ellison, Ph.D. and John L. Genz, M.P.A., *Stress and the Police Officer* (Springfield: Charles C Thomas, Publ., 1983), p. 9.

3. Ellison and Genz, pp. 10, 11.

4. *Stress Management,* lecture notes, Federal Bureau of Investigation, National Academy, Quantico, Virginia, 1985. (*Note:* Academic courses at the F.B.I. National Academy were accredited by The University of Virginia—this applies to all subsequent notes.)

5. James T. Reese, "Life in the High-Speed Lane: Managing Police Burnout," *The Police Chief,* June 1982, p. 49.

6. Reese, p. 49.

7. James T. Reese, "Workshop/Stress and Its Control," *The Police Chief,* March 1983, p. 111.

8. Reese, "Life in the High-Speed Lane," p. 50.

9. Reese, "Life in the High-Speed Lane," p. 50.

10. Reese, "Life in the High-Speed Lane," p. 50.

11. Reese, "Life in the High-Speed Lane," p. 50.
12. *Stress Management*, lecture notes.
13. Ellison and Genz, p. 27.
14. Ellison and Genz, pp. 28, 29.
15. Ellison and Genz, p. 27.
16. Carol A. Martin, "Workshop/Stress and Its Control," *The Police Chief*, March, 1983, p. 107.
17. *Stress Management*, lecture notes.
18. Ellison and Genz, pp. 28, 29.
19. Reese, "Life in the High-Speed Lane," p. 49.

Chapter IV
BODY AND HEALTH

1. Wm. H. Kroes and J. Hurrell, *Job Stress and the Police Officer*, U.S. Department of Health, Education and Welfare, (NIOSH), 1975, p. 1.
2. Kroes and Hurrell, p. 1.
3. William L. Proudfit, M.D., "The Heart and Circulation," *New Family Medical Guide* (Des Moines: Meredith Corp., 1982), p. 41.
4. Herbert G. Langford, M.D., "Hypertension," *New Family Medical Guide*, p. 71.
5. Wm. H. Crosby, M.D., "The Blood," *New Family Medical Guide*, pp. 89, 90, 92.
6. Jess R. Young, M.D., "Blood Vessel Disorders," *New Family Medical Guide*, p. 79.
7. Robert D. Fazzaro, M.D. and L. Fred Ayvazian, M.D., "The Lungs," *New Family Medical Guide*, pp. 157–163.
8. *Holistic Fitness and Nutrition*, lecture notes, F.B.I. National Academy, Quantico, Virginia, 1985.
9. Nathan Pritiken, *The Pritiken Promise* (N.Y.: Simon & Schuster, 1983), p. 99.
10. *Stress Management*, lecture notes, F.B.I. National Academy, Quantico, Virginia, 1985.
11. Wm. D. Carey, M.D. and Richard Farmer, M.D., "The Liver," *New Family Medical Guide*, p. 463.

Chapter V
LIFE–STYLE DEATHS

1. Richard Bocklet, " 'Steady Tours' Get Enthusiastic Response," *Law and Order*, February 1988, p. 54; *Cited as 53 Years*. Also, William H. Kroes, Ph.D., *Society's Victims — The Police* (Springfield: Charles C Thomas, Publ., 1985), p. 133; *Cited as 59.22 Years* (Ref. to: Delaware State Police Retirees). Also, *1967 Occupation Study* (Chicago: Society of Actuaries, 1967), pp. 40, 41; *Cited as 59 Years*. Also, John F. Reintzell, *Analysis of Deaths: The Baltimore Police Department's Retirement System — Years 1984-1986* (unpubl.): *computed at 60.5 Years*. Also, John M. Violanti, "Obesity — A Police Health Problem," *Law and Order*, April 1985; *Citing (Guralnick 1963) as 59 Years*.
2. W. R. Spence, M.D., "Life Styles and Causes of Death" (Waco: Spenco Medical, 1985), p. 2. "Each year Americans spend over $100 billion on medical bills,

futilely trying to patch up their abused bodies. In spite of this, the American male stands in approximately 40th place in world longevity rankings. Why? The answer lies in a comparison of our twelve leading causes of death and our life styles. . . . "

3. Bocklet, Kroes, Society of Actuaries, et al.
4. Nathan Pritiken, *The Pritiken Promise* (N.Y.: Simon & Schuster, 1983), p. 14.
5. Herbert G. Langford, M.D., "Hypertension," *New Family Medical Guide* (Des Moines: Meredith Corp., 1982), pp. 71–74.
6. Langford, pp. 71–74.
7. Langford, p. 71.
8. *The Surgeon General's Report on Nutrition and Health* (Summary), U.S. Department of Health and Human Services, 1988, p. 13.
9. *The Surgeon General's Report on Nutrition and Health*, p. 13. Also, Langford, p. 73.
10. William L. Proudfit, M.D., "The Heart and Circulation," *New Family Medical Guide*, p. 63.
11. Proudfit, p. 65.
12. Proudfit, p. 65.
13. Kenneth H. Cooper, M.D., M.P.H., *The Aerobics Program For Total Well-Being* (N.Y.: Bantam Books, 1982), p. 96.
14. Denise Foley, "Clean Out Your Cholesterol," *Prevention*, July 1985, p. 36.
15. Proudfit, p. 65.
16. Proudfit, p. 64.
17. Kenneth H. Cooper, M.D., M.P.H., *Running Without Fear* (N.Y.: M. Evans & Co., 1985), p. 91.
18. Dean Ornish, M.D., *Stress, Diet and Your Heart* (N.Y.: Holt, Rinehart and Winston, 1982), p. 16. "Following coronary bypass surgery, the blockages in the coronary arteries tend to become progressively worse and even the bypass grafts can become clogged, often requiring additional surgery."
19. Violanti, p. 59.
20. Michael B. Shimkin, M.D., "Cancer," *New Family Medical Guide*, p. 699.
21. Shimkin, p. 699.
22. Shimkin, pp. 703–706.
23. "Advance Report of Final Mortality Statistics, 1986," *Monthly Vital Statistics Report*, U.S. Department of Health and Human Services, Vol. 37, No. 6 Supplement, pp. 29, 30.
24. Shimkin, p. 703.
25. Shimkin, p. 708.
26. Shimkin, p. 700.
27. John S. Meyer, M.D., "Stroke (Vascular Disease of the Brain)," *New Family Medical Guide*, p. 237.
28. Meyer, pp. 237, 241.
29. Meyer, p. 237.
30. Meyer, p. 237.
31. Meyer, pp. 237–239.
32. Meyer, p. 237.

33. *Holistic Fitness and Nutrition* lecture notes and course material.
34. "Births, Marriages, Divorces, and Deaths for January 1990," *Monthly Vital Statistics Report,* U.S. Department of Health and Human Services, Vol. 39, No. 1, pp. 14, 15. Also, *Holistic Fitness and Nutrition* lecture notes and course material.
35. Katherine W. Ellison, Ph.D. and John Genz, M.P.A., *Stress and the Police Officer* (Springfield: Charles C Thomas, Publ., 1983), p. 27; Citing Monat & Lazans, 1977).
36. Robert D. Fazzaro, M.D. and L. Fred Ayvazian, M.D. "The Lungs," *New Family Medical Guide,* p. 178.
37. Fazzaro and Ayvazian, pp. 178–179.
38. Aldo A. Rossini, M.D., "Diabetes Mellitus," *New Family Medical Guide,* p. 389.
39. Rossini, p. 389.
40. Rossini, pp. 395–396.
41. Rossini, pp. 389, 393.
42. Cooper, *The Aerobics Program,* p. 95.
43. Proudfit, p. 62.

Chapter VI
NUTRITION

1. *The Surgeon General's Report on Nutrition and Health* (Summary), U.S. Department of Health and Human Services, 1988, p. 18.
2. Kenneth Cooper, M.D., M.P.H., *The Aerobics Program For Total Well-Being* (New York: Bantam Books, 1982), p. 76.
3. Nathan Pritiken, *The Pritiken Promise* (New York: Simon and Schuster, 1983), p. 54.
4. *The Surgeon General's Report on Nutrition and Health,* p. 10.
5. Cooper, p. 65.
6. Marcia Seligson, "Nutrition," *Esquire,* May 1984, p. 146.
7. John M. Violanti, "Obesity—A Police Health Problem," *Law and Order,* April 1985, p. 60.
8. Michael Brown, "Fast Foods are Dangerous To Your Health," *Science Digest,* April 1986, p. 31.
9. Cooper, p. 92.
10. *The Surgeon General's Report on Health and Nutrition,* p. 10.
11. Cooper, p. 92.
12. Values As: Cheeseburger, 37. Regular Fries, 9. Milkshake, 32, or 78 mg. of Cholesterol (Furnished by McDonald's).
13. Richard Demak, "Heart Attack and Cholesterol," *Discover,* March 1984, p. 21.
14. Pritiken, pp. 16, 17.
15. Pritiken, p. 19.
16. Pritiken, p. 34.
17. Pritiken, p. 54.
18. Pritiken, p. 34.
19. Pritiken, p. 54.

20. *Holistic Fitness and Nutrition,* lecture notes, F.B.I. National Academy, Quantico, Virginia, 1985.
21. Pritiken, p. 55.
22. Pritiken, p. 55.
23. Pritiken, p. 16.
24. *The Surgeon General's Report on Health and Nutrition,* p. 18. In part, *"Health Professionals:* Improved nutrition training of physicians and other health professionals is needed. Training should emphasize basic principles of nutrition, the role of diet in health promotion and disease prevention. . . . "
25. Pritiken, p. 15.
26. *The Surgeon General's Report on Health and Nutrition,* p. 12.
27. Pritiken, p. 33.
28. *Holistic Fitness and Nutrition,* course material.
29. Seligson, p. 146.
30. Howard Jacobson, M.D. and J. Timothy Hesla, M.D., "Nutrition," *New Family Medical Guide,* p. 444.
31. Cooper, p. 65. "The reason for this is not entirely clear. Perhaps if you take in most of your food early in the day you can process it more readily."
32. Pritiken, pp. 16–20.

Chapter VII
BODY FAT

1. Kenneth H. Cooper, M.D., M.P.H., *The Aerobics Program For Total Well-Being* (N.Y.: Bantam Books, 1982), p. 65. "I am convinced that if you consume the largest proportion of your calories before 1:00 p.m. you will have less of a problem controlling your weight than if you consume the same number of calories *after* 1:00 p.m. . . . "
2. *Holistic Fitness & Nutrition* course material, F.B.I. National Academy, Quantico, Virginia, 1985.
3. Nathan Pritiken, *Permanent Weight Loss Manual* (N.Y.: Grosset & Dunlap, 1981). "In fact, most overweight people, including people who have been overweight since childhood, have a normal number of fat cells but an abnormal amount of fat in those cells. These people can easily achieve normal weight."
4. Nathan Pritiken, *The Pritiken Promise* (N.Y.: Simon & Schuster, 1983), p. 99.
5. Cooper, p. 71.
6. Bailey, Covert, Address delivered at Southern California Dental Convention, 1978, p. 4.
7. Nathan Pritiken, *The Pritiken Promise,* p. 99.
8. Pembrook, Linda, *How to Beat Fatigue* (Garden City: Doubleday & Co., 1975), p. 58.
9. Pembrook, p. 57. Also, "Police Urged To Improve Physical Fitness," LEAA Newsletter, Vol. 6, No. 5, 1976, p. 12. "The most frequent cause was heart-related . . . the second was back trouble. . . . "

10. *The Surgeon General's Report on Nutrition and Health* (Summary), U.S. Department of Health and Human Services, 1988, p. 5.

11. "Girth and Death," Statistical Bulletin, *Metropolitan Life*, Vol. 18, May 1937, pp. 2–5. Obviously, knowledge of this relationship has been around for *many* years.

12. Bailey, p. 10.

13. Cooper, p. 71.

14. Cooper, p. 73. The factors, 15 or 13 are "if you want to get maximum energy — without gaining any weight...." "For example, if you are involved exclusively in sedentary activities, such as office work without any outside exercise, you should multiply your ideal body weight by 15 or 13, according to whether you're under or over 40."

15. *The Surgeon General's Report on Nutrition and Health* (Summary), U.S. Department of Health and Human Services, 1988, p. 5.

16. Pritiken, *The Pritiken Promise*, p. 99.

17. Pritiken, *The Pritiken Promise*, p. 99.

18. Geoffrey Cannon and Hetty Einzig, "Does Dieting Make You Fat?", *Reader's Digest*, December 1986, p. 135.

19. Nathan Pritiken, *Permanent Weight Loss Manual*, pp. 13, 14. Also, Cannon and Einzig, p. 135.

20. Cooper, p. 75.

21. Cooper, p. 75.

22. Cooper, p. 70.

23. Cooper, p. 75.

24. Cannon and Einzig, p. 135.

Chapter VIII
ALCOHOL

1. Leon Dishlacoff, "The Drinking Cop," *Stress and Police Personnel* (Boston: Allyn and Bacon, Inc., 1981), p. 115.

2. *Stress Management*, lecture notes, Federal Bureau of Investigation, National Academy; Quantico, Va., 1985.

3. John G. Stratton, Ph.D., *Police Passages* (Manhattan Beach: Glennon Publ. Co., 1984), p. 250.

4. James R. Milam, Ph.D. and Katherine Ketcham, *Under The Influence* (New York: Bantam Books, 1983), p. 27.

5. Milam and Ketcham, p. 19.

6. Milam and Ketcham, p. 21.

7. Milam and Ketcham, pp. 22, 23.

8. Milam and Ketcham, pp. 27, 35.

9. Milam and Ketcham, pp. 43–45.

10. Milam and Ketcham, pp. 39–42.

11. Milam and Ketcham, p. 27. Indeed, recovering alcoholics often are prescribed

the drug Antabuse (TM) which blocks the liver's ability to eliminate acetaldehyde. This causes a severe and immediate toxic reaction.

12. Milam and Ketcham, p. 56.
13. Milam and Ketcham, pp. 34, 35, 54. Acetaldehyde, an intermediate by-product of alcohol metabolism, "appears to be one of the major villains in the onset of alcoholic drinking." Studies confirm that "the breakdown of acetaldehyde is performed at about half the rate of 'normal,' i.e. non-alcoholic metabolism." This slowdown allows the toxic material to accumulate.
14. Milam and Ketcham, p. 28.
15. Milam and Ketcham, p. 28. "In alcoholics up to two-thirds of the body's total energy needs may be satisfied by substituting alcohol for other foods. This explains why alcoholics often neglect eating for several weeks at a time."
16. Milam and Ketcham, p. 23.
17. Milam and Ketcham, p. 29.
18. Katherine W. Ellison, Ph.D., and John L. Genz, M.P.A., *Stress and The Police Officer,* (Springfield: Charles C Thomas, Publ., 1983), p. 46.
19. Milam and Ketcham, p. 189.
20. *Stress Management,* lecture and course materials.
21. *Stress Management,* lecture and course materials.
22. *Stress Management,* lecture and course materials.
23. Ellison and Genz, p. 27.
24. Roger Vogler, Ph.D., and Wayne R. Bartz, Ph.D., *The Better Way To Drink* (Oakland: New Harbinger Publ., 1982), p. 36.

Chapter IX
ALIENATION

1. *Stress Management,* lecture notes, F.B.I. National Academy, Quantico, Virginia, 1985.
2. Michael J. Asken and David C. Raham, "Resident Performance and Sleep Deprivation," *Journal of Medical Education,* Vol. 58, May 1983, pp. 384, 385.
3. Katherine W. Ellison, Ph.D., and John L. Genz, M.P.A., *Stress and The Police Officer* (Springfield: Charles C Thomas, Publ., 1983), p. 68. In part, "they are cast into limited stereotypic roles and pressured by male peers to remain subordinate through a variety of verbal and non-verbal cues. [They] adopt two patterns of behavior . . . one group succeeds as officers by a strategy of overachievement. . . ."
4. Ellison and Genz, p. 68 and " . . . invisibility and strict adherence to the rules. . . . "
5. John G. Stratton, "Pressures in Law Enforcement Marriages: Some Considerations," *Stress and Police Personnel,* Territo & Vetter, Eds. (Boston: Allyn & Bacon, Inc., 1981), pp. 234–238. Also, Paul E. Mott, "Social and Psychological Adjustment to Shift Work," *U.S. Department of Health, Education and Welfare,* 1976, p. 149.
6. Stratton, p. 237.
7. *Stress Management,* lecture notes.

Chapter X
BODY RENEWAL

1. John M. Violanti, "Obesity: A Police Health Problem," *Law and Order,* April 1985, p. 6.
2. *Heart Care,* The American Medical Association Home Health Library (N.Y.: Random House, 1982), p. 59. Citing The University of California's Ralph S. Paffenberger [who] "found strong statistical evidence that an individual's heart attack risk diminishes if he engages in strenuous sports such as swimming, running, basketball, handball, squash or tennis." (See my comments regarding *tennis!*)
3. *Heart Care,* p. 59. Also, mentioned in Kenneth H. Cooper, M.D., M.P.H., *Running Without Fear* (N.Y.: M. Evans & Co., 1985), p. 186.
4. Kenneth H. Cooper, M.D., M.P.H., *The Aerobics Program For Total Well-Being* (N.Y.: Bantam Books, 1982), p. 83.
5. Nathan Pritiken, *The Pritiken Promise* (N.Y.: Simon & Schuster, 1983), p. 125.
6. *Pritiken, p. 125.*
7. Cooper, *The Aerobics Program,* p. 94.
8. Cooper, *The Aerobics Program,* p. 144. Dr. Cooper's book includes charts which assign "aerobic fitness points" to various physical activities. He suggests that you "average" 27–32 points a week." For a person 30–49 years of age that equates to walking three miles four times a week in under forty-four minutes per workout; or running/jogging two miles each four times a week in 20–22 minutes per workout.
9. *Holistic Fitness and Nutrition* lecture notes.
10. Pritiken, p. 99. "If walking is to be your form of exercise, figure 400 calories expended in one brisk hour's walk covering four miles. Joggers will be expending 600 to 900 calories in the same time."

    However, a runner will do three miles in twenty-seven minutes *or less,* thus burning *270* calories or 45% of what the walker burns: i.e. 600–900 calories × .45 = 270 to 405 calories.

    Cooper, *The Aerobic Program,* p. 122. Though he concludes running will burn calories more efficiently than walking, he also writes, "But there is one exception to this generalization: in between the twenty-minute walk and the 6:15 mile run, there is a progressive *increase in calorie cost for walking and a decrease for running.* Additionally, he wrote "and at the energy-cost 'threshold' between walking and running—or the point where the energy expended in running slowly and walking at a fast pace tended to converge—we *discovered that the oxygen cost for walking a mile in twelve minutes was actually higher than it was for running a mile at that speed"* (emphasis mine). Therefore, you will probably burn more calories walking a mile than running a mile!
11. Bailey, Covert, Address delivered at Southern California Dental Convention, 1978, p. 4.
12. Cooper, *The Aerobics Program,* pp. 113–119. Also, Pritiken, pp. 16–22.

13. *Holistic Fitness and Nutrition,* lecture notes.
14. Bailey, Covert, *Fit or Fat?,* Boston: Houghton Mifflin, 1977, p. 22.
15. Pritiken, p. 54, and Bailey, pp. 18, 19.
16. Pritiken, p. 18.
17. Pritiken, pp. 17, 18.
18. Cooper, *The Aerobics Program,* pp. 192–197.
19. Bailey, p. 91.
20. *Holistic Fitness and Nutrition,* lecture notes.
21. *Holistic Fitness and Nutrition,* lecture notes.
22. *Holistic Fitness and Nutrition,* lecture notes.
23. Cooper, *The Aerobics Program,* p. 90.
24. Cooper, *The Aerobics Program,* p. 90.
25. Cooper, *Running Without Fear,* p. 80.
26. Cooper, *The Aerobics Program,* p. 287. The range is:

Fitness Category	*Average*
Very Poor	6.06
Poor	5.66
Fair	5.14
Good	4.86
Excellent	4.28

Chapter XI
HOLISTIC LIFE–STYLES

1. Dean Ornish, M.D., *Stress, Diet & Your Heart* (N.Y.: Holt, Rinehart and Winston, 1982), p. 16. Dr. Ornish writes, "Most medical interventions occur after the fact, when a person already has become sick. Medical technology is usually channeled into treating rather than preventing coronary disease. Unfortunately, in subtle and not so subtle ways, medical students and residents often are taught that patients do not become 'interesting' until after they have developed a disease."
2. *The Surgeon General's Report on Nutrition and Health* (Summary), U.S. Department of Health and Human Services, 1988, p. 18.
3. *Stress Management,* lecture notes, F.B.I. National Academy, Quantico, Virginia, 1985.
4. *Stress Management,* lecture notes.
5. *Stress Management,* lecture notes.

SELECTED REFERENCES

PERIODICALS/ARTICLES

1. Asken, Michael J., Ph.D., and David C. Raham, M.D., "Resident performance and sleep deprivation: a review," *Journal of Medical Education,* May, 1983.
2. Bocklet, Richard, " 'Steady' duty tours get enthusiastic response," *Law and Order,* February, 1988.
3. Brown, Michael H., "Fast foods are hazardous to your health," *Science Digest,* April, 1986.
4. Cannon, Geoffrey, and Hetty Einzig, "Does dieting make you fat," *Readers Digest,* November, 1986.
5. Carey, Joseph, and Joanne Silberner, and Erica D. Goode, "Fending off the leading killers," *U.S. News & World Report,* August 17, 1987.
6. Czeisler, Charles A., Martin C. Moore-Ede, and Richard M. Coleman, "Rotating shift work schedules that disrupt sleep are improved by applying circadian principles," *Science,* Vol. 217, July 30, 1982.
7. Davis, Paul O., Ph.D., and Albert R. Starck, M.A., "Age vs. fat," *FBI Law Enforcement Bulletin,* September, 1980.
8. Debro, Julius, Dr., "Stress and its control: a minority perspective," *The Police Chief,* March, 1983.
9. Dodge, Robin, "Circadian rhythms and fatigue: a discrimination of their effects on performance," *Aviation, Space, and Environmental Medicine,* November, 1982.
10. Edelson, Edward, "Preserving the breath of life," *The American Legion Magazine,* August, 1985.
11. Foley, Denise, "Clean out your cholesterol," *Prevention,* July, 1985.
12. Hall, Barbara Green, "Prescription for police stress: talk to your wife," *Police Stress,* February, 1982.
13. Krajick, Kevin, "Out of shape on the beat," *Police Magazine,* May, 1979.
14. LaDou, Joseph, M.D., "Health effects of shift work," *The Western Journal of Medicine,* December, 1982.
15. Langone, John, "Heart attack.and cholesterol," *Discover,* March, 1984.
16. Leonard, George, "Life skills," *Esquire,* May, 1984.
17. Logan, Daniel, "Physical fitness training and the police department," *Universal Fitness Products,* 1973.
18. Maleskey, Gale, "All about triglycerides," *Prevention,* March, 1986.
19. Metropolitan Life, "Girth and death," *Statistical Bulletin,* Vol. 18, May, 1937.

20. Monthly Vital Statistics Report, "Advance Report of Final Mortality Statistics. 1986," Vol. 37, No. 6, Supplement, September 1988.
21. Monthly Vital Statistics Report, "Births, Marriages, Divorces, and Deaths for January 1990," Vol. 39, No. 1, May 1990.
22. National Safety Council, "Recordable occupational injury and illness incidence rates, 1982–1984, by industry, reporters to the National Safety Council. Cont.," *Accident Facts*, 1985.
23. "Police urged to improve physical fitness," *LEAA Newsletter*, Vol. 6, No. 5, 1976.
24. Reese, James T., "Family therapy in law enforcement," *FBI Law Enforcement Bulletin*, September, 1982.
25. Reese, James T., "Life in the high-speed lane: managing police burnout," *The Police Chief*, June, 1982.
26. Reintzell, John F., "Sleep deprivation, police stress and a prescription" (Unpubl.) 1984.
27. Shepherd, Jack, "Aerobics," *Esquire*, May, 1984.
28. Smith, Gerald M., M.Ed., and Francis R. Dunphy, Ed.D., "Health/fitness and professional education: an innovative course at the FBI Academy," *FBI Law Enforcement Bulletin*, August, 1987.
29. The Stanford University, "Guide to a healthier heart—academy series," *Prevention*, February, 1986.
30. Thompson, Paul D., M.D., and Amby Burfoot, "Eat to live," *Runner's World*, September, 1986.
31. Violanti, John M., "Obesity: a police health problem," *Law and Order*, April, 1985.
32. Webb, Wilse B., and C. Michael Levy, "Age, sleep deprivation, and performance," The Society for Psychophysiological Research, Inc., 1982.

BOOKS

1. Bailey, Covert, *Fit or Fat?* Boston: Houghton Mifflin, 1977.
2. Cooper, K. H., *The Aerobics Program For Total Well-Being*. New York: Bantam Books, 1982.
3. Cooper, K. H., *Running Without Fear*. New York: M. Evans and Company, 1985.
4. *Crime in the United States*, Federal Bureau of Investigation, U.S. Department of Justice, Washington, D.C., 1987.
5. Ellison, K. W., and John L. Genz, *Stress and The Police Officer*. Springfield: Charles C Thomas, Publisher, 1983.
6. Gasner, D., and Elliott H. McCleary, *Book of Heart Care*. New York: Random House, 1982.
7. Girdano, D. A., and George S. Everly, Jr., *Controlling Stress and Tension*. Englewood Cliffs: Prentice-Hall, 1986.
8. Jacobson, Michael, *The Fast Food Guide*. New York: Workman Publishing, 1986.
9. Johnson, Leanor B., Ph.D., Veronica F. Nieva, Ph.D., and Michael J. Wilson, Ph.D., *Police WorkHome Stress Study Interim Report, 1985*. Westat, Inc., 1985.
10. Kiester, E., Jr. (Ed.), *New Family Medical Guide*. Des Moines: Meredith Corporation, 1982.

11. Kroes, W. H., *Society's Victims — The Police.* Springfield: Charles C Thomas, Publisher, 1985.

12. Kroes, W. H., and J. Hurrell, *Job Stress and The Police Officer.* U.S. Department of Health, Education and Welfare, 1975.

13. Milam, J. R., and Katherine Ketcham. *Under The Influence.* New York: Bantam Books, Inc., 1983.

14. Moore-Ede, Martin C., Frank M. Sulzman, and Charles A. Fuller, *The Clocks That Time Us.* Harvard University Press, 1982.

15. 1967 Occupation Study, *Society of Actuaries.* Chicago, 1967.

16. Ornish, Dean, *Stress, Diet & Your Heart.* New York: Holt, Rinehart and Winston, 1983.

17. Pritiken, Nathan, *The Pritiken Permanent Weight-Loss Manual.* New York: Grosset & Dunlap, 1981.

18. Pritiken, Nathan, *The Pritiken Promise.* New York, Simon & Schuster, Inc., 1983.

19. Rentos, P. G., and Robert D. Shepard (Eds.), *Shift Work & Health.* U.S. Department of Health, Education, and Welfare, Washington, D.C., 1976.

20. Smith, R. S., *Nutrition, Hypertension & Cardiovascular Disease.* Gilroy: The Lyncean Press, 1984.

21. Stratton, J. G., *Police Passages.* Manhattan Beach: Glennon Publishing Company, 1984.

22. *The Surgeon General's Report on Nutrition and Health,* U.S. Department of Health and Human Services, Washington, D.C., 1988.

23. Territo, L., and Harold J. Vetter, *Stress and Police Personnel.* Boston: Allyn and Bacon, Inc., 1981.

24. *The Union Memorial Hospital Human Performance Lab,* Baltimore City Police Fitness Assessment Results, Baltimore, Maryland, 1987.

25. Vogler, R. E., and Wayne R. Bartz, *The Better Way to Drink.* Oakland: New Harbinger Publications, 1982.

26. Wojtcak-Joaszowa, Jadwiga, *Physiological and Psychological Aspects of Night and Shift Work.* U.S. Department of Health, Education and Welfare, Cincinnati, 1977.

INDEX

131